MORE CAJUN HUMOR

Other Books by Justin Wilson

The Justin Wilson Cook Book (1965)
Justin Wilson's Cajun Humor (with Howard Jacobs) (1974)
The Justin Wilson No. 2 Cookbook: Cookin' Cajun (1979)
Justin Wilson's Cajun Fables (with Jay Hadley) (1982)
Justin Wilson's Gourmet and Gourmand Cookbook (1984)

MORE CAJUN HUMOR

by JUSTIN WILSON
with HOWARD JACOBS

PELICAN PUBLISHING COMPANY
GRETNA 1985

This book is dedicated to all those peoples who have learned to laugh at themselves.

Library of Congress Cataloging in Publication Data

Wilson, Justin.
More Cajun humor.

I. Jacobs, Howard. II. Title.
PN6162.W543 1984 818'.5402 84-7087
ISBN 0-88289-454-4

Manufactured in the United States of America
Published by Pelican Publishing Company
1101 Monroe Street, Gretna, Louisiana 70053

Foreword

Drive an hour from New Orleans in any direction and you will find yourself in another world. This world may be called Thibodaux, Chauvin, Pointe-a-la-Hache, Maurepas, Broussard, or Mamou. It has a language that is not English, yet not quite French. It has different customs, its own cuisine, and a point of view that you won't find anywhere else. This is the Cajun world—a world created by the same God, but blessed far beyond all others.

Cajun is the shortened form of the word *Acadian,* which described a group of native French people who lived in Canada in an area around the Bay of Fundy. In 1755 the Acadians were evicted from their homes, separated from their families, and herded aboard ships by the British. These ships eventually deposited some hearty survivors along the Gulf Coast, mainly at the bays and river mouths of South Louisiana. The Cajuns dispersed themselves deep into the swamps or rode up the bayous until they found land far from any authority, where they began to work and live.

It was a life free of the city but inseparable from the land and water, animals and plants they found all around them. As they prospered, they held on to their language and philosophy. They were mostly Catholic. Family and friends were the most important ingredients in their recipe for life. They worked hard and then enjoyed their free time to the fullest. They loved to laugh.

Cajun humor is gentle humor. Cajuns tell stories on themselves; they don't care who a joke is on, just so there is a joke. They are not offended by ethnic humor, because they think everybody else is ethnic. Cajun humor is full of stories of animals, stories of hunting and fishing, stories of drinking and dancing at the local barroom-saloon, stories of children getting the better of adults, wives getting the better of husbands, and braggarts being brought down to the common level. And since Cajuns think everyone else talks funny, confusion or a play on words results when the languages don't quite connect. Cajuns love to laugh at themselves, because they know that they are funny as hell.

Justin Wilson is at home in the Cajun world. He is half Cajun—a half-bleed, he says. Son of a remarkable Cajun mother and a witty Welsh father, he has lived among Cajuns all his life. For the last fifty years Justin Wilson has been telling the rest of the world about his world: telling them about how it was and how it still is in a few places like Lafayette, French Settlement, St. Martinville, Maringouin; telling them to laugh at themselves; and telling them how to have the fun that Cajuns have.

Bienvenu au monde Cajun!

JEANNINE MEEDS WILSON

MORE CAJUN HUMOR

Group Insurance

I got a frien' w'at got hisse'f hurted once an' he was in de horse-pistol. An' one o' dem peoples w'at sold dem group insurance stuff brought hisse'f to de horse-pistol to see him. He say, "I'm glad for you to see me, I ga-ron-tee."

Dat insurance salesman say, "I'm glad for you to see me, too, 'cause I wan' to talk to you."

Ma' frien' say, "I wan' to talk to you, too, but you ma' gues' so you go 'head."

He say, "You know dat group insurance stuff I sol' you?"

Ma' frien' say, "Sho' I know, I put up ma' money."

De fallow say, "Well, I hate to tole you dis, but de whole damn group got to get hurted befo' it can be some good."

Old Man Noah and the Big Flood

Las' year 'roun' April, we had a pretty bad flood 'roun' dair where I live until finally de water start recedin' isse'f down.

An' dair was a Sunday School teacher in a li'l Baptis' church talkin' wit' her pupils, an' she say, "Chirren, we not goin' to have our regular Sunday school, no. I'm goin' to talk 'bout ol' Man

Noah an' de big flood." One li'l girl say, "Noah's flood worser den dis, hanh?" An' she say to de li'l girl, "Much worser."

She say, "Ol' Noah was tole to buil' a how-you-call h'ark." De chirren say, "W'at a h'ark is, hanh?" "Oh," say de teacher, "Dass a boat wit' lid on top." "Chris-Craft?" ax a li'l boy.

"No," say de teacher. "He was tole to build dat h'ark on top a high mountain. An' Noah dues jus' w'at he was tole. He got dat boat built, an' den come de voice, 'Noah, you got to brought you'se'f out dair an' got a pair of avery kind of animule, bird an' fish an' reptile, an' fill dat ark. An' not lookalikes, no. Jus' pairs.'

An' den it began to rain—not buckets, but carloads—for forty day an' night. Den all of a quick it jus' ended like dat. So dey float 'roun' dair fo' a couple o' weeks, an' Noah notice de food is runnin' out, an' de animules might start eatin' each odder if dey don' watch out. So he sent out a dove (dass a homin' pigeon). Dat dove stay out dair a hour an' a half, den brought hisse'f back all tuckered out, an' jus' make it back to de deck o' de boat. He was 'mos' out o' breathe. But he don' brought not'ing back wit' him.

"W'at dat mean?" ax de teacher. "Tijon, you know?"

"You got de wrong mans, I don't know, me," Tijon say. Den li'l Marie jomp up an' say, "I know, I know w'at it mean. It mean he didn't find land."

"Dat's r'at," the teacher say. "Den Noah dispatch anodder dove, an' dis one didn't brought hisse'f back, none a-tall, any."

"I know w'at dat mean," Tijon say. "It mean dat dove season done open' in Sout' Lewisana."

Alligator Shoes

I got a frien' dat one day was talkin' wit' a bunch o' us an' he say, "You know, ma' ol' lady, she say, 'W'en you gonna get me some alley-gator shoes, hanh? How come you don' get me some alley-gator shoes? I need some alley-gator shoes. Please get me some alley-gator shoes.' "

He say, "I hear dat in ma' sleep, she say it so much. 'W'en you gonna get me some alley-gator shoes? I need some alley-gator shoes.' "

"De odder day I was rode down de road in my country Cadillac an' a six-feet alley-gator cross dat road in fron' o' me, goin' into de marsh. An' I pull dat truck to a dead still an' reach down an' pull my immer-gency broke so it won' roll an' dat alley-gator wen' in dat swamp an' me r'at behin' him.

"I chase him five mile t'rough dat swamp befo' we get to a place dat is open enuf fo' me to get wit' him. *Flip, flap, flip, flap, bloom,* he 'mos' beat de hell f'om me wit' his tail. But after a while I wear him down mo' den me, an' I turn dat alley-gator on his back, an' you know, he ain't got on one damn shoe."

False Alarm

Down in Crowley, Lewisana, years ago when I lived down dair, dey had a barbershop where you could get a shave, an' I never will fo'got one day dair was a man in de barbershop who was laid out on de chair. De barber got all dat white cloth draped over him wit' a little pin at de back o' his neck, an' got his face covered wit' a hot towel, steamin' his face.

A man rushed in an' grabbed him by de shoulder an' say, "Boudreaux, you' house is on fire down de street," an' he jomped from dem barber chair, jerked dem towel f'om his face, an' ran 'bout fo' or t'ree blocks down de street an' all of a sudden, he brought hisse'f to a dead still.

He say, "W'at de hell I'm runnin' fo"? In de secon' place, I don't even got no house. An' in de firs' place, ma' name ain't Boudreaux."

Big Texan—Little Cajun

Not long ago, in fac' jus' las' winter, dair was a Cajun talkin' to a Taxan who was not too well-eddicated. De Taxan, I mean. Either he did not know or he done hauled off an' forgot dat de United States done took in Alaska. He tole dat Cajun how big Taxes was, the bigges' of averyt'ing in de United States, de bes' of averyt'ing, an' he wasn't 90% r'at in averyt'ing he was sayin' to him, excep' Taxes was not de biggest. But he kept on tellin' him, an' avery time dat Cajun tried to say somet'ing, *shoom,* he cut him off short.

Dat Cajun say, "Look, we got some water hyacinth in Lewisana dat's pretty an'—" An' dat Texan say, "Yeah, but we got bluebonnets dat will cover 'em up an' planty fast." An' it keep on like dis, an' dat pore li'l Cajun could not get a word in wit' a wedge.

But dat big Taxan pause to take a breathe an' dat li'l Cajun say, "We got one t'ing in Lewisana you ain't got in Taxes, I ga-ron-tee." De Taxan say, "W'at dat is?" He from Port Arthur, you know.

De Cajun say, "We got de Mississippi River in Lewisana an' you ain't got not'ing like dat in Taxes, I ga-ron-tee!" Dat Taxan say, "You know, you r'at, an' dat's de only t'ing you got in the whole state of Lewisana dat I wish we had in Taxes. I'd give anyt'ing in de worl' if we had de Mississippi River in Taxes, I tell you fo' sho'."

De Cajun say, "You mean dat?"

He say, "Of course I mean dat, I would not have said it if I didn't mean it."

"Well, hokay," de Cajun tole him. "W'en spring brought isse'f, we gonna buil' a pipeline from de Mississippi River to Houston, Taxes, an' if you Taxans can suck in jus' one-tenth o' w'at you can blow out, you'll have it in t'irty secon's, I ga-ron-tee!"

Cajun Confusion in the City

Not long ago, dair was a Cajun frien' wit' me dat took hisse'f to New Or-lee-anhs for de firs' time. He got off de train in the New Or-lee-anhs station an' he walked across de street an' he looked down from the bank o' de gutter an' dair's somet'ing green fold up down dair an' he reach down an' pick it up an' it's money. He say, "Look at dis. Money." He count it out an' it's $8.34. He say, "Now ain't dat nice. Dey welcome you to New Or-lee-anhs wit' money like dat."

'Bout dat time here come one o' dem streetcars an' he ain't never seen like dat befo' ag'in in his life an' it stop an' he get on dair. An' he's so proud 'cause he got some money—he didn't have much w'en he got down dair. He rode along dair and he come to Poydras Street an' dat conductor holler, "Poydras." Two men got up an' get off dat streetcar an' dat Cajun say, "Well, w'at you t'ought 'bout dat? Dat conductor know dem men name and call 'em so dey get off at de r'at place. W'at you t'ought 'bout dat?"

Dat conductor go some mo' further and he holler, "Iberville," an' three mo' men got off. Ma' frien' say, "Well, I jus' can't unnerstood a man know all o' dem peoples like dat." Nex' corner, "Bienville," an' fo' men got up and ma' frien' say, "Now you know, he know all dem peoples." A li'l bit further, "Peters," an' a man an' a female woman get up an' get off. He say, "Look, he know bot' de husban' an' his wife. I never seen a man like dat so smaht befo' ag'in in ma' life."

Dey go jus' a li'l bit further an' de conductor yell, "Broussard," an' he say, "Well, dat's me. W'at you t'ought about dat? How he know me like dat?"

Well, he get up an' get off de streetcar an' he's standin' dair an' a auromobile drove itse'f up an' dair's two men in de car an' one o' dem say, "Broussard?"

Broussard say, "Dat's r'at."

De man say, "834?"

He jus' reach in his pock-ett an' han' 'em de $8.34 r'at now.

The Cajun from Texas A&M

I got two frien's live nex' door to each odder outside o' Bat-onh Rouge, an' dey got each one dem small garden. Now iss too small fo' one dem tractor, so dey bought an' ol' mule to work bot' o' dem. An' one day dey was sittin' on one o' dey porch, sippin' pop wit' foam on top an' some o' dat good Cajun whiskey from Tennessee call Jacques Dan-yell. Now dis mule was stoodin' dair wit' ears droopin' an' one dem fallow say to de odder, "You know, we got to buil' a stall fo' de mule, hanh?" "Dass r'at," his frien' say. "After dis rain stop, we gonna did dat."

So dey built a stall fo' de mule, but he balked w'en dey tried to put de mule in dair, an' one dem fallow say, "You know w'at wrong? Dat mule's ears are too long fo' dat stall. So we got to trim 'em off."

So one o' dem got a straight razor, an' de odder one got some axle grease, but de mule don' how-you-call cooperate, an' he give dem fallow a bad time. Pretty soon a young fallow walk up, de nephew o' one o' dem, an' watch dem try to cut off de tips of de mule's ears. But after dat stubborn mule kept pullin' away an' backin' off, de nephew suggested, "Why don' you buil' a trench in de stall fo' de mule?"

After de nephew lef', de two farmers try summore, an' finally one o' dem say, "You know, dey never did taught dat boy in college dat you don' have to buil' a trench to trim a mule's ears."

Essence of Contempt

You know, Livingston Parish where I live is a wondermus parish—de free state of Livingston. An' dey had a judge dair who fined a man $25 for contempt of court. De judge say, "I fine you $25 fo' contempt of court. You got anything to say to de court?" He say, "Hell yeah. It was wort' avery damn penny of it."

Abundant Squirrels and a Super Rabbit Dog

I was sittin' here makin' some talk an' I got to t'inkin' 'bout ma' good frien' Murphy Brown. He's a full-bleed Cajun even t'ough his name is Murphy Brown. Dis is true. He live down in Whitehall near Maurepas, Lewisana. An' Murphy loves to hont.

An' 'bout t'ree week ago, I was at a political meetin' wit' him an' he come up to me an' say, "Juice-tanh, you gonna hont squirrel wit' me dis year?"

I say, "Murphy, are dair many squirrel dis year?"

He say, "De woods is full o' 'em. In fac', dey sleepin' on de groun', 'cause dair ain't enuf room in de trees."

I say, "Murphy, de season open October 4 an' rabbit season open de same day. After we go out an' got dem squirrel, you reckon we could go got a few rabbit? You got a good rabbit dog?"

He say, "Have I got a good rabbit dog? *Whoo!* You ax a damn fool question like dat! I got a dog dat is so good I got to cover up one nose wit' tape to keep him f'om chasin' two rabbit at one time."

Flailee

Years ago in Lewisana, we use to have a lot o' good boxin' in de high schools. Boy, I want to tole you it was somet'ing. I use to go to all dem fights. I even referee a couple o' dem, got de hell knock out o' me. 'Cause w'en dem youn' boys is flailin', dey don't care who dey flailin' on, you year? An' I been de flailee a couple o' times.

An' I never will fo'got dey had de state turnamen' in Mamou. Had a fine boxin' team, an' dey had an ol' boy dat would fight averybody in town but he did not know how to box. But he always ax de coach, "Coach, lemme get in dair an' fight. Gimme a chance, Coach, gimme a chance, hanh, hanh, hanh?" "Oh," de coach say, "you don' know how to fight." "Oh, hell yeah, I can fight." De coach say, "Well, I got a good heavyweight. I don' want to mess up t'ings."

Well, dey had de turnamen' an' Coach Winsdale's—he not from Mamou, he can't speak no Franch—his prize heavyweight got sick. He sent for dis fallow and say, "You wan' to fight?" He say, "Hell yeah, I ga-ron-tee!" De coach say, "A'r'at, get in dair an' fight. I hate like hell to forfeit de fight!"

Well, dat odder fallow like to beat him to deat'. He was t'rowin' dem gloves at him by de basketful. An' he come by de coach an' he say somet'ing in Franch, an' de coach say, "Get in dair an' fight!"

He come ag'in an' say somet'ing mo' in Franch an' de coach say to one o' de secon's, "W'at he said?"

De secon' say, "Coach, if you don' t'row dat towel in dair soon, he gon' jomp dat li'l ol' t'ree-stran' barb-wire fence, I ga-ron-tee!"

Just in Case

I got a frien' w'at's a used car dealer in Opelousas, Lewisana. One day a good-lookin' female girl lady womans brought herse'f to his used car lot an' say, "You got some foreign-made auromobiles, hanh?"

An' de dealer say, "You come to de r'at place, you. We got averyt'ing excep' de way to manufacture 'em. We don't make 'em up—dass all."

She say, "Howse 'bout dat red car over dair?"

He say, "Dass fine. It's made in Detroits, Mitchigan. Can't get no more foreign den dat."

She say, "Well, me, I don' know not'ing some a-tall 'bout dem foreign cars."

"Don' worry, bêbe," ma' frien' say. "Me, I got knowledge for de bot' o' us."

"Well, show me dem car. I don' know somet'ing none a-tall 'bout foreign auromobiles."

He put her in de car an' she say, "Whoo! Jus' look at dem dashin'-board."

He say, "You see dat gauge r'at cheer? Dass you' gasoline gauge. An' dat big *E* dair don' mean 'evermore,' no. It mean 'empty.' Now dat *F* mean 'fun an' play.' Fool 'roun' all you want."

"W'at 'bout dat li'l black knob?" she say.

"Never min', I'll come 'roun' to dat. Now dis gauge r'at cheer tells w'ether you' car is charge or decharge. You' alteration, you' generation. An' dis gauge tell how hot you are."

"W'at you said?"

"Dat red mark r'at dair. Needle get dair, you better stop at a fullin' station or a bayou an' pull you' radiation up, 'cause you got too hot wit' you' auromobile."

She say, "I wanna know 'bout dat li'l black knob."

"We'll get to dat," he say. "On de steerin' while, you see dat li'l lever dair. Dass you' turnin' predictor. It tells which way you gonna turn, if you don' changin' you' min'."

"Me, I still wanna know 'bout dat li'l black knob."

"Well," he say. "Dass a *justin case.* Dass a choker, an' you don' need a choker in dis climate."

"Well, how come dey put it dair, hanh? All you say is 'Justin case, justin case, justin case.' "

He tore his shirt open to reveal bare chest.

"Look," he say. "I got two breast but I ain't gonna have some chirren. So dey put dem on, *'justin case.'* "

Mail Service

I got a frien' w'at live in Kaplan, Lewisana—dat's in Vermilion Parish. He's a trapper, him. He also too besides is a guide fo' dem big shoots in Taxes w'at come over dair to shoot dem dock. An' trappers make big money, yeah. Lewisana produces more fur den Canada—mos' peoples don' realize dat. He's got to take de big shoots to de blin'. Den he's got to stay wit' dem, 'cause dey couldn't find de way back. An' somebody got to kill dem dock, too.

Now he been hearin' all about Las Vegas, Nevada, from de big shoots. One day he say, "W'at 'bout Las Vegas, Nevada?" "Why," say one o' de big shoots, "dass de gamblin' capital o' de worl'."

"More den Lewisana?"

"Oh, hell yeah."

He say, "Me, I got to go dair." But one o' de big shoots say, "Look, man, you got to take money. You got to have $40,000 in cash befo' you can go out dair. It'll take you ten years to save dat up!"

But dey don' know 'bout dem trapper, an' in six mont' he done save 'bout $50,000, an' Uncle Sam didn't know beans 'bout it. He takes one dem fas' arrow-plane non-stop to Vegas. Got dair an' registered. But he hadn't been dair long befo' fas' womens an' slow horses did him in.

"Lemme see if I got any money to got back to Lewisana," he say to hisse'f. He paid his hotel bill, an' found he didn't have enuf lef' to tip de bellboy.

So he say to de bell captain, "Look, you need a good, strong man here?"

He say, "No, but dey're hiring peoples at de pos' office." So ma' frien' walk down de street an' ax de postmaster 'bout a job. "Oh," say de postmaster, "we need a mail sorter bad, I ga-ron-tee!"

"You're lookin' at de vary bes'," he say, all de time wonderin' w'at de hell a mail sorter was.

So de postmaster brought him in de back an' showed him all de bins w'at dey got dair. "We been fallin' behin' in our separatin'," he say. He left de man dair an' took off fo' a couple o' hours. Soon de new mail sorter was hummin' on de double, "Ta rah rah boom yee yea—ta rah rah," all de time flailin' his arms an' sendin' dem letters into de bins lickety-split.

"Man," de postmaster ent'used w'en he come back. "You de fastes' mail sorter I aver did see."

An' de new mail sorter say, "If I could read, I'd be twice as fas'."

Room Service

I never will fo'got one time I had to brought mase'f to a big town and I go up to the desk where dey got a clerk behin' dair, you know, in de hotels and I say, "Ma' frien', I got a reserve here."

He say, "W'ats you' name?" I say, "Front name or behin' name?" He say, "Bot' names," an' I tole him.

He say, "How you spell dat?" 'Cause he don' unnerstood dem good Anglish, you know, and I spell it fo' him an' I'm so proud 'cause I jus' learn how to did dat, you know.

He say, "Let me look on de book," and he get de book an' he t'umbed t'rough it real fas'. He say, "I don' see you name." I say, "Well, slow youse'f down, how you gonna look dat fast?" I say "Let's start dis t'ing over an' I'll be glad to help you look."

He say, "Okay," an' turn one page. I say, "Stop youse'f r'at dair. Dair's ma' name." He say, "Dat's r'at but you got to wrote you name in de register." I say, "Put 'em out cheer." He put 'em out dair an' I'm printin' ma' name real careful 'cause some people can read readin' but dey can't read writin'—you know how dat is. An' jus' when I get t'rough, the biggest doggone bedbug I never see ag'in in ma' life walked r'at across ma' name.

Whoo, dat put me hot, I ga-ron-tee! An' I back up fo' or t'ree step an' I say, "Ma' frien', look, I wanna tole you somet'ing. I been bit by de flea in Shrevepo't, I been bled by de spider in Bat-onh Rouge, an' I been chased by de police in New Or-lee-anhs. But dat's de firs' time I ever had a bedbug look up ma' room number in ma' life, I ga-ron-tee you dat!"

Key to Problem

You know, lady an' gentlemans, de true story are always de one dat make me feel mo' better an' good. An' several year ago, I lived in de town o' Crowley, Lewisana, de rice capital o' de worl'. It been quite a few several year ago. W'en I lived dair, dey had a fire depahtment dat was kine o' volunteer an' t'ings like dat.

Now I was in a barroom saloon cocktail loonge drinkin' a glass of buttermilk an' dair was a Cajun stood at de bar dair an' he was dronk, *oohh,* I'm talk about he was some dronk. His front name was William but dey called him "Bill" for short, you know. He had a bottle of beer by the neck holdin' real tight, an' dat's w'at held him up. He would rock back an' fo'th wit' dat bottle of beer but he don' fall. An' we was all sittin' 'roun' dair drinkin' dat buttermilk an' dat pop wit' foam on top an' de fire whistle blow f'om de cou'thouse at Crowley. Well, averybody jomp up an' get dey pocketbook an' get dey li'l card out w'at tell you how many blows an' dat tell you r'at where de fire is.

Well, we check dem an' it don't blow our place so we sit ou'se'ves down. An' dat Cajun jus' stan' up dair—Bill jus' stan' dair an' don' leave dat bottle of beer some a-tall. He jus' hol' on an' real good. 'Bout dat time, all two fire engines in Crowley brought demse'ves by wit' dey syringes wide open, full blas'. An' averybody run outside to see which way dey goin', excep' Bill, he don' lef' dat bottle, he jus' hol' on real good. So we seen dem go where we t'ought dey was gonna go. Dey turn de corner an' we brought ou'se'ves back an' sit down. Bill jus' stan' r'at dair. In a few minnits, one o' his frien's brought hisse'f in an' he say, "Bill." Bill say, "Dat's w'at dey call me, ma' man."

His frien' say, "Bill, don' you got some shame on you'se'f, hanh? To stood up here dronk like dat, hanh?"

Bill say, "Hell no. It took me six week to get like dis."

He say, "Bill, you mean to tole me you stan' up here dronk like dis. Don' you hear dem fire whistles blow up dair at de cou'thouse, hanh?"

Bill say, "Me, I don't care if dey blow f'om de cou'thouse all de way. I don't give a damn, me."

He say, "Bill, I'm so 'shamed o' you, I don't know w'at to do. You mean to say you don' see dem fire engines pass dis place jus' den, hanh?"

Bill say, "I don' care if dey go t'rough dis place. Jus' so dey don' knock dis bottle of beer f'om ma' han'."

He say, "Bill, I'm so 'shamed o' you I jus' don' want to spoke wit' you summore. You stan' up here dronk like dis an' you' house burnt up r'at down dair on de corner. I'm 'shamed o' you."

Bill say, "W'at in de worl' wrong wit' you, ma' frien'? How in de hell my house gon' burn up? I got de key r'at cheer in my pock-ett."

Duckology

You know, I got a frien' w'at is a guide down in de dock-hontin' country in Sout' Lewisana, an' one day one of dose rich Taxans brought hisse'f over dair to hont dem dock. He got two case of shell wit' him an' two ah-romatic shootgun. Now a ah-romatic shootgun is one w'at got one hole an' shoot t'ree time from de same hole if de game warden is dair, an' if he ain't, it shoot five time r'at in de same place.

An' de Taxan get dis guide dair an' he spend de night at his camp. De nex' mornin' dey load all de Taxan shell—de limit is fo' dock—an' dey take bot' gun case. An' dat guide go an' get one shell he got on de top shelf dair—10-gauge. An' he got a one-hole gun—it don't shoot but one time. He get dat shell an' put it in his pock-ett an' dat big shoot from Taxes say, "Dat all de shell you gon' took?" De guide say, "Dat's all I need."

De Taxan say, "But I'm shootin' 12-gauge an' you shootin' 10."

Ma' frien' say, "Dat's a'r'at. Dis one shell is enuf fo' me. Less go."

So dey get in de pirogue boat an' dey get in de blin' an' man, ma' frien' call dem dock, *quanh, quanh, quanh, quanh, quanh,* an' he dued de feed call an' he put 'em r'at down dair. An' dis big shoot from Taxes, he get bot' dem gun so hot, you can't stan' to hold 'em. An' he get de limit, an' he run out o' shell.

An' he say, "Less go. We got de limit." Ma' frien' say, "No, I wanta shot dis one shell I got wit' me." He say, "Go ahead an' shot it."

De guide say, "No, I got to get it jus' r'at."

Here come a huge big flock o' dock. An' dat guide, *quanh, quanh, quanh, quanh, quanh,* he call 'em an' good. *Quanh, quanh, quanh,* he give 'em dat feed call an' w'en dey jus' 'bout to lan', he raise up wit' dat ol' one-hole 10-gauge an' *bloom!* Dock fall averywhere. *Plip, plop, plip, plop, plip, plop.* He got out dair an' he say, "Come he'p me pick 'em up." Dey go out dair an' dair's fo'ty-nine dock.

Dat big shoot Taxan say, "Less go."

Ma' frien' say, "No, dair's one mo' dock out dair."

An' dey look an' dey look, an' dat Taxan say, "Look, dair ain't no mo' dock out dair. Less go."

Ma' frien' he say, "Oh, hell yeah, dair's one mo' out dair."

De Taxan say, "Well, how you know?"

He say, "Well, dair's fifty BBs in dat shot an' we don't got but fo'ty-nine dock."

An' 'bout dat time, dey look an' here come a dock swimmin' fas' as he can, wit' dat li'l shot r'at behin' him.

Cajun Cow-Calling

You know, lady and gentlemans, not long ago I was down at Port Vincent in a barroom saloon cocktail loonge drinkin' buttermilk. You laugh, but dat's de trut'. An' dair was a man in dair an' he came up to me—he was not drinkin' buttermilk. An' he say, "Juice-tanh." (Dat's ma' name in Franch.) An' I say, "W'at dat is?" He say, "You talk 'bout a cow, I got a cow."

I say, "W'at kine o' cow you got, ma' frien', hanh?" I was bein' nice an' I'm interested in farmin' an' all dat.

He say, "Well, less see. Her ma-ma was t'ree-quarter Jersey an' her pa-pa was t'ree-quarter Jersey, so dat make her a Jersey an' a half, I ga-ron-tee."

Young Couple in Auto

Not long ago, down on de road where I live between Denham Springs an' French Settlement, Lewisana, I was goin' down dat road one day, name Pete's Highway, named for a ol' Frenchman name Pete Comeaux who used to go see his frien' girl. She mus' have made the bes' home brew 'cause dat road is laid out on de road he took an' dat road is crooked, *whoo!*

But I was drivin' dat road not long ago, an' I was behin' a

auromobile in which was a young couple an' dey was sittin' up close, close, close, like a sick kitten to a hot brick, you know. An' dis boy was drivin' dat auromobile an' doin' two job, you know. Dey was sittin' up dair close, close like dey was bot' deaf an' all o' a sudden, *brump, brump, brump, brump, brump,* an' dat girl look at him an' she say, "Honey, I hate to tole you but I bleeve we got a flat tire."

He say, "You don't mean to tole me."

She say, "I ga-ron-tee. We better stop an' look at dat."

He say, "Hokay."

Well, he stop de car an' he get out an' look an' dey got a flat tire. He change de tire an' get back in de car an' *brump, brump, brump, brump, brump.*

Dat fool done change de wrong tire!

Astrodome

Not long ago, down in French Settlement dair where I live—I talk 'bout it quite a bit 'cause it is such a wonderful place an' dey got some wonderful people down dair who are of French descent an' a few of Spanish descent dat de Cajuns absorb w'en dey got in dair an' let me tell you, dey absorb 'em r'at quick.

But we got some down dair dat have de most beautiful accent in dis worl' name Murphy an' Henderson—dis is true—'specially one frien' who I love to hear him talk name Murphy Brown. Murphy's got it, I ga-ron-tee.

One day I was down dair, t'ree or two mont' ago, an' I was talkin' to Murphy an' he ax me, he say, "Juice-tanh." I say, "W'at dat is?"

He say, "Have you ever been to Houston, Taxes, hanh?"

I say, "I ga-ron-tee."

He say, "Tole me about dat."

I say, "Ain't no way. 'Cause averyt'ing I tole you, you swear iss a damn lie, an' so I ain't 'bout to tole you. You got to go dair to see dat."

He say, "I wish I could go." He ain't never been but twenty-five mile from home ag'in in his life. An' I tole him, I say, "I'll took you."

He say, "I'll go."

So we made arrange. He wanted to go r'at den but I say, "No, less wait. I got to pack a suitcase. Dat ain't all. I want to fine out w'en de Astros are playin' bessball. I hope dey play de day we are dair."

So we fine out w'en dey home an' we go over dair an' we go to dat Astrodome an' I sit down an' wait for him 'cause he got to look at averyt'ing an' he do, 'specially dat cute li'l girl in de miniskirt w'at took him 'roun'.

An' we go to one o' de res'rants w'at dey got in de Astrodome—dey got a lot o' nice ones dair—an' we go dair an' eat launch befo' de ballgame.

An' w'en we get t'rough dat cute li'l female girl lady waitress woman brought de check over dair an' gave it to me. I reach in ma' pock-ett to get somet'ing to leave on de table for her an' I don't have anyt'ing.

So I tole him, I say, "Look, leave somet'ing on de table for dat cute li'l waitress."

He say, "Hokay."

Now I get up an' take de check an' go over to de cashier an' I pay de check. An' I wait for him at de do'.

W'en he get dair, I ax him, "Did you leave somet'ing on de table for dat cute li'l waitress?"

He say, "You damn r'at. I ga-ron-tee I did. I lef' dem ol' carrots. I never could stood dem t'ings."

Cajun Astrolo-Jest

Not long ago in a li'l town in Sout' Lewisana—I'm not gonna say where dis was, 'cause dis could have been in Nort' Lewisana—dey was two Cajuns in a barroom saloon cocktail loonge an' dey he'p close it up 'bout t'ree o'clock in de mornin'.

An' dey walk out o' dair an' *whoo!* dey dronk. Dey so dronk dey don' know dey wholesale from dey retail—an' dass bad. An' dey get out in fron' an' dey stan' on de street dair an' dey get to argue 'bout which way de sun brought isse'f up.

One o' dem say, "De sun brought isse'f up in de west, averybody know dat."

De odder one say, "You don' know w'at de hell you talk 'bout. Averybody know de sun brought isse'f up in de east."

An' dey got a big argue. "Oh no, de west." "Oh no, de east." "You don' know somet'ing anyt'ing a-tall." "Iss de east dat it brought isse'f up in."

So dey go on 'bout t'irty or twenty-five minnits an' dey see anodder Cajun brought hisse'f up de street dair an' he's in pretty bad shape, too. In fac', he on his han's an' knees to make it. One o' dem say, "Look, w'en he get hisse'f here, we gonna ax him to settle dis argue, an' w'atever he say, dat's w'at we gonna accep'. If he say de sun brought isse'f up in de east, dat's hokay. If he say de west, dat's hokay too. How 'bout dat?"

De odder one say, "Hokay." Well, dis Cajun finally crawled up dair an' dey grab one arm on each side an' dey lift him up an' dey say, "Look, we got a big argue. Me, I say de sun brought isse'f up in de west an' he say it brought isse'f up in de east. It brought isse'f up in de west, hanh?"

De odder one say, "Look, don' pay some 'tention wit' him. I say it brought isse'f up in de east an' he say it brought isse'f up in de west. It brought isse'f up in de east, don' dat r'at, hanh?"

Dat dronk Cajun look at him an' say, "Don' ax me. I don' live 'roun' here."

Chaos in Church

Dair was two Cajun lived down in Livingston Parish. Dair is also a community called Oilfiel' dair an' of cou'se dair's de parish seat called Livingston an' in between dair's a church. An' dis happen years ago befo' anybody had a auromobile an' averybody had to ride a horse an' buggy. Dair was a man name Emile an' he was a very fine man. He sang in de choir at church an' wen' to church avery Sunnay. Now jus' because he go to church don' make him a fine man. He a good fallow w'ether he go to church or not. An' dair was a fallow name Jacques an' he was a good man for not'ing. I mean plum' good for not'ing. He didn't give a damn, him; if cabbage ever came to a head, he figurin' to live off o' turnips. He was sacrilegious an' averyt'ing else, you know.

An' one day Jacques lef' Oilfiel' goin' to Livingston, an' it was cloudy. An' Emile, he lef' Livingston headed for Oilfiel'. An' he saw it was goin' to rain so he jog up his horse a li'l bit an' he got to dat church which was 'bout halfway between dose two place.

Well, Emile put his horse in de shed, go in de church, get up in de choirbox, an' pick up a hymn book an' sat dair readin' a hymn book.

An' man, dat t'understorm came up an' it caught Jacques real good. He rode in fron' o' dat church, jus' like Roy Rogé—dat Cajun Cowboy, you know. He rode up dair an' he got off dat horse, ran up dair an' open dat do', go in dair an' say, "Hello, dair, Lord."

An' Emile say, "Hello, Jacques." An' *shoom!* Jacques ran r'at back out dat do'—dat do' didn't even get a chance to close!

I was talkin' wit' a frien' wit' me, an' he say, "You know, dat story is true. I live a mile from dat church an' I look out dair dat day an' here come ol' Jacques runnin' in fron' o' dat horse, leadin' dat horse, I ga-ron-tee!"

The Lamb Who Thought He Was a Dog

You know, I got to tole you 'bout ma' frien' Travis Lobell, who live in Springfield, Lewisana, an' got a big schicken farm. A half-million layin' hens, now you know, dat's somet'ing, hanh? He also, too, got hogs, sheeps, an' cattle. An' he got one ol' sheep dat had twin lambs. She didn't want to have not'ing to do wit' one o' dem, but she raise de odder one.

So Travis's two cute li'l daughters took dat li'l lamb to de house an' fed it on de bottle. Dey also had two lickin' pot houn's dat dey was raisin' an' befo' too long, dat li'l lamb t'ought he was a dog. He would eat wit' dem dogs an' sleep wit' dem. W'en dey chase auromobiles, he would too. He would even go hontin' wit' dem dogs. Well, I got a kick out o' watchin' dat lamb, I really did. Avery time I wen' over dair, I would mos' kill ma'se'f laughin' 'bout dat lamb.

One day I was dair an' I didn't see de lamb an' I ax Travis, "Where dat lamb is, hanh?"

He say, "Oh, I had to kill it."

"W'atever fo'?"

He look at me an' shake his head. "It start killin' sheep."

Tennis Shoes

'Bout a year ago, dair was a Cajun who stood at a fullin' station down dair on I-10 down in Sout' Lewisana between Lafayette an' de Taxes line. An' a fallow drove up dair in one o' dem fas'back auromobiles w'at look like *shoom,* it been cut off wit' a broadax.

An' dis Cajun walk over dair an say, "Dass a nice lookin' car you got dair."

De fallow say, "Yeah, go 120 mile an hour."

De Cajun say, "I can run dat fas'."

De fallow say, "Oh, yeah, w'at kine o' car you got, hanh?"

De Cajun say, "I don' need a car. I'm talkin' 'bout me."

Dat fancy-car fallow say, "I don' bleeve dat."

Dat Cajun say, "You callin' me a lie?"

An' de fallow, he say, "No, I jus' doubt you' word, dass all."

So de Cajun say, "A'r'at, less get out dair on de interstate an' I'll show you."

(An' I wan' you peoples to know dat was befo' we got dat new superintendent of police down dair, too.)

So dey get out dair an' dis fallow don' want to embarrass dat Cajun. He put his foot on de acceleration an' go up to 35 mile a hour an' he look out dat side window an' dair dat Cajun is, runnin' 'long side o' him lightin' a cigarette.

Dat fancy fallow say, "I can't stood dis." He put his foot down on de acceleration summore, up to 55 mile a hour, an' he look out dat window. Dat Cajun done t'row dat cigarette away an' unwrap a piece o' bubble gum and POP, put dat in his mout', jus' runnin' 'long dair, jus' joggin' 'long.

De fallow say, "Well, I'll show him," an' he put his foot on de acceleration to 75 mile a hour. He look out dair an' dat Cajun runnin' along dair blowin' a great big bubble wit' dat bubble gum.

De fallow say, "You don' mean to tole me dis. I'll show him for sho an' r'at now." So he put his foot all de way on de acceleration an' go 120 mile a hour an' SHOOM, he gone. He look out dat window an' dat Cajun runnin' 'long beside him an' real good.

He look back at dat road 'cause you got to watch dat road w'en you go 120 mile a hour, you know. He look back out dat window and dat Cajun gone. He say, "I wonder w'at happen wit' him."

He foun' a place to turn 'roun' on dat interstate—dat take a li'l while—an' he go back an' look on dat center median to dat las' place he saw dat Cajun.

An' dair dat Cajun is on dat center median, jus' one big brushburn from head to feets, I ga-ron-tee.

He say, "W'at in de worl' happen wit' you, hanh?"

Dat Cajun say, "You ever had a tennis shoe blow out goin' 120 mile a hour, hanh?"

Would You Believe

Down off o' Gran Ile—dat's Grand Isle to you peoples way up nort'—dis Cajun tole me dey was down dair tryin' to catch some fish. Dey caught a fish dat was so doggone big dat dey tried to get him in de boat, an' all dey could do was get him up close to de boat an' dey finally jus' roped him wit' block an' tackle an' hol' him good an' wen' to shore.

An' dey got a winch dump truck wit' a gin pole on dair an' dey had to get a big one. An' dey hook on to dat fish an' dey pick him up out o' de water. An' den dey look fo' scales to weigh him. An' dey took all kine of pitcher. An' dey couldn't fine a scale big enuf to weigh de damn t'ing, you know. So dey took anodder pitcher an' I wan' you to know dey weigh de pitcher an' it weigh eight an' t'ree-quarter poun's. De pitcher did. Dat's some fish, hanh?

Dat's kine o' like dat frien' wit' me, tole me de odder day, "I got de mos' wondermus, eddicated bird dog in de worl' an' de U.S. an' A., too."

I say, "Well, I got some pretty good dogs mase'f. Dey can retrieve dem bird—dey fine 'em an' poin' 'em an' averyt'ing else."

Ma' frien' say, "Well, you jus' don' know, dis one is de bes' in de worl'."

I say, "How come iss so good?"

He say, "Well, I wan' to tole you. If you wan' come an' go hontin' wit' me, I'm gon' tole you w'at you do now. Dass de bes' t'ing you can do an' you can see fo' you'se'f. If dat dog retrieve a bird fo' you, now, you got to watch dat dog real close. Real close, close, close, watch dat retrievin' bird dog w'at I got. W'en he retrieve dat bird, he goin' to look up at you an' you have bot' eye on him, 'cause if he wink at you like dat, he done pick up a cripple bird. An' he goin' to wink at you an' drop dat bird an' if you don' watch real close, dat bird gon' get away, you year?"

Catfish Joe

You know, I got a frien' name Catfish Joe who not long ago was fishin' down near where I live on de Amite River wit' anodder frien' an' he tole me 'bout dis.

He say, "Man, we was fishin' out dair an' ma' frien' was fishin' an' *whoo,* did he git a bite. It 'mos' drug him in de river, you year? In de bayou he 'mos' wen' an' I say, 'Don't los' him, you year?' I say, 'He is a big one. Dis is de one we been fishin' fo' all our life. Hang on to him.'

"He say, 'Don't you worry. I got him.'

"An' he kep' tryin' to get dat fish, an' all o' a sudden he tole me, he say, 'Joe, I hate to tole you, but I bleeve we hung on somet'ing down dair unner de water.'

"I say, 'Well, jus' hol' you'se'f still. Don' los' him. I'll dive down dair an' see w'at go on.'

"You know, I dive down dair an' follow de line all de way to de bottom. An' somebody done park a auromobile r'at dair on de bottom of dat river.

"An' I look in dat auromobile an' I see w'at goin' on. He done hang a 52-poun' blue channel catfish. An' I can tole he weigh dat much an' he ain't got scale on him one, you year?

"I come up close an' I can see we hang up on somet'ing in dat auromobile. An' you know, when I reach in dair to untangle dat line, dat damn catfish roll dem window up on dat auromobile!"

Sobriety Test

Not long ago in Bat-onh Rouge, dair was a policemans cop on his way home from shift change. It was 'bout 'laven o'clock an' he was on his way to de house, an' he got to double back de nex' mornin' at saven, an' all he wan' to do is get home an' get on de bed, an' r'at now.

An' he was on his way an' here come a Cajun in his car and he don' miss one damn inch of dem road. De policemans say, "*Boy*, look at dat!! Now, if I took him downtown and put him in dat jail, it gon' take me t'ree or two hour to get home. I wonder if maybe I straighten him up an' talk wit' him an' maybe I could go on home." So he turned his red light, blinkety, blinkety, blinkety, on him an' turned his syringe on full blas', an' dat Cajun pulled hisse'f over dair an' dat policeman stop an' say, "Get from de car."

Well, he stepped out o' de auromobile an' you know how a dronk will do, he try to stan' up straight an' he stan' so straight he 'mos' fall over back'erds. An' de policemans say, "Are you dronk?" He say, "Who?"

"You," de policemans say, "dat's de only one I see 'roun' here." "Oh," he say, "hell no, I ain't dronk."

Well, like I tole you, he don' wan' to took him down dair to dat jail. He say, "Look, I wan' to tell you somet'ing. I'm gon' give you a chance to prove you not dronk." Dat Cajun say, "Hokay, less go, boy."

De policemans say, "You see dat five-stran' barb-wire fence r'at over dair, hanh?"

De Cajun say, "Yeah, one, two, t'ree, fo', five, dat's r'at, five stran's."

He say, "If you can jomp dem five stran's barb-wire an' not touch 'em wit' anyt'ing, an' den jomp back, maybe you not too dronk an' I'll let you go."

Well, dat Cajun jus' kinda walked up to dem fence and *bloom,* he jomp over. W'en he get in dat pasture, here come a great big white Brahma bull, an' dat Cajun dronk an' he turn 'roun' and see dat bull bear down on him an' he grabbed him by bot' horns, one horn in each han', an' *kerbloom, blip,* stick bot' dem horns in de groun' an' walked up to dem fence and *bloom,* jomp over dair, an' dat policemans say, "Well, you jomped it an' good, but w'at in de worl' was goin' on in dem pasture dair, hanh?"

Dat Cajun say, "Look, if dair's anyt'ing I can't stood, iss for somebody to try to run over me on a bicycle."

The Well-Prepared Football Spectator

You know, lady an' gentlemans, I love de game of football. In fac', I coached it one year, an' dass all we gon' say 'bout dat.

I love to go see de games. I love to see action on de fiel' dat Howard Cosell don't have sense enough to put de camera on. In doin' dat, I have seen a lot o' football fans in ma' lifetime an' avery section t'inks iss got de greates'. In fac', Taxes jus' *know* dey got de greates'.

But de mos' savage, rabid, avid, hydrophobic, utter football fans in de worl' is de Lewisana Cajun who live on de bayous an' rivers of Sout' Lewisana. Dey bleeve in 'em so much dey bet on a replay, you know dat? An' dey support de Tigers of L.U.S.

Savarel year ago, de Tigers were to play dat girls' school in Sout' Ben', Indiana, how-you-call de Frightened Irish of Notre Dame. Dair must have been twelve t'ousan' o' us Cajuns wen' along to he'p 'em as much as we possible could. A whole bunch o' ma' frien's w'at live on de Mississippi River in Paulina, Lutcher, Garyville, an' Vacherie go dair. We wen' to dat hotel call de Palmer House.

Nex' mornin' we got up to go to de game an' we foun' out iss sixty mile, plum', to go to de stadium. So ma' frien's an' mase'f rented a bus.

W'en we out dair, a big Cajun from Lutcher hel' up two tickets an' say, "I got ma' tickets, I ga-ron-tee."

"Oh," I say, "you brought you' ol' lady?" He say, "Hell no. She don' unnerstood dat game like me."

I say, "Who you brought? I ain't gon' tell nobody." He say, "Nobody. Dese two ticket fo' me."

I say, "Look, I know somebody need a ticket bad, bad, bad. W'at de hell you gon' did wit' dose two ticket?"

An' he say, "Well, I'm goin' up dair in dat stadium an' yell like hell fo' L.U.S. An' one dem damn Yankee gon' start a fight wit' me an' I'm gon' fight back. An' dey gon' t'row me out o' dat stadium an' I need dis odder ticket to got back in."

The Long, Long Football Field

You know dey used to play all de high school games down on de Mississippi River an' some o' de places in Sout'wes' Lewisana on Sunnay. But w'en de Oilers got a football team, dey quit playin' in Sout'wes' Lewisana on Sunnay. Dey start playin' on We'nesday so dey could see de Oilers play. An' in Sout'eas' Lewisana, dey quit playin' on Sunnay so dey could go see de Saints play on Sunnay—or *try* to play, I mean.

An' I don' know w'ether dese two Cajuns were talkin' bout de

Saints or de Oilers, but one o' dem say, "You know, I know w'at's wrong wit' dem. Dey givin' de signals away."

"W'at de hell you mean, 'Give de signals away'?" de odder one say.

"You go to de games?"

"Hell, yeah, I go to de games."

"You know w'en dey come out o' de huddle, t'ree o' dem backfiel' men are laffin' like hell, an' one o' dem is pale as a ghost."

Years ago, Opelousas, Lewisana, had a coach name Faize Mahfouz an' he was a real fine high school football coach, I ga-ron-tee. I wish he was still in de business. Opelousas had a real fine football club an' were t'inkin' 'bout winnin' de state champinship. Dey had a halfback name Randy Brown who was de vary bes', you year? *Whoo boy!* Greas' lightnin'!!

An' Opelousas play New Iberia an' dey was sepose to beat de hell f'om dem, all de way, plum', an' de tar, averyt'ing you beat f'om peoples. But dey don' did dat, no. Dey tie 'em—not'ing-not'ing.

Well, dis on Sunnay an' all de chirren was dair, averybody was dair. Tie-tie. Not'ing-not'ing. Dey figurin' on Faize to win, gon' come back an' celebrate. No classes hardly a-tall, jus' goin' in an' have fun.

Dey get back an' ain't none o' dem got dair lessons. Dey jus' stan' 'roun' in class. An' de firs' class wit' de coach an' dey know he mad like hell anyhow. One o' dem say, "You get you' lessons?" "No, hell no. I didn't get 'em. You?" "No."

Somebody say, "W'at somebody ought to did is ax de coach w'at happen." One boy say, "I'll be damn, I ain't ax him." A li'l girl say, "I'll ax him." "Go 'head on," de boy say, "Coach like girls. You ax him."

So dey get in de class an' de coach got in an' *shoom,* she put her han' up. Cute li'l girl. Faize say, "W'at you want, darlin'?" She say, "Coach, w'at in de worl' happen wit' us an' New Iberia?" He say, "I'm glad you ax dat." (An' dat's a damn lie 'cause he was not glad.)

An' he wen' t'rough all de whole game an' de t'ings w'at happen dair in de football game. An' he say, "I wan' you chirren to know somet'ing. Randy Brown gain 306 yards on de groun' by hisse'f" (an' dis is a matter of record, lady an' gentlemans) "an' he did not score."

A li'l boy in de back raise his han' up an' Faize say, "W'at you want, son?"

He say, "You mus' o' been playin' on a long fiel', hanh?"

The Fisherman

I got a couple o' frien's w'at was fishin' down dair near where I live—I like fishin' stories 'cause I like to fish an' don' get near enuf chance to do it as I would like to—an' dey were in a bateau five feet wide. Dat's a wide boat you can walk aroun' in if you want to. An' dey had a couple of coolers wit' dem wit' pop wit' foam on top an' dey had some o' dat Cajun whiskey wit' dem too—Jacques Dan-yell.

An' dey got out dair an' dey fished an' fished an' fished an' not one bite did dey get, excep' mosquitoes, dass all. An' dey was drinkin' dat pop wit' foam on top an' dat Jacques Dan-yell, an' de firs' t'ing you know, dey was dronk an' feelin' real good. An' dey was jus' 'bout to los' dere discourage an' one o' dem say, "Look, less don' los' our discourage. I'm tole you w'at I'm gon' did. I bet you five dollar I'm gon' catch de firs' fish."

Ma' odder frien' say, "You got a bet an' r'at now." An' he reach in his pock-ett to get a five-dollar bill an' he lay it in de boat, an' he was tryin' to get dat change w'at he had grab wit' de five-dollar bill back in his pock-ett an' he fell overboard.

W'en he brought hisse'f to de top o' de water, spittin' half o' de river out, fumin' an' sputterin' all at de same time, de odder frien' look at him an' say, "If you gonna start divin' fo' dem r'at now, all de bets are off, I ga-ron-tee!"

The Little Man

Dis is a true story about a li'l boy who was five year ol' an' he wanted so bad to be grown up like all li'l boys do an' den w'en dey grown up dey want to act like chirren. An' avery Sunnay mornin' after de usual Satiddy nite parties, his ma-ma an' pa-pa wen' out to breakfas'. An' dey took him wit' 'em. Dey had a regular routine ritual fo' doin' dis.

An' he wen' wit' 'em one Sunnay mornin', jus' like a li'l man, an' he always wanted to order his own breakfas'. An' dis pa'ticular Sunnay mornin', he tole his ma-ma an' pa-pa, he jus' talk wit' 'em so nice, "Please, ma-ma, let me order ma' own breakfas', please, please, lemme, hanh?" She look at her husban' an' he say, "Hokay."

An' de waitress stan' dair, nice li'l female lady waitin' fo' him, an' she say, "W'at would you like for you' breakfas'?"

He say, "I wan' some orange juice, some bacon, an' agg."

Dat waitress look at him an' say, "How would you like you' agg, hanh?"

He say, "On de rock!"

Cajun Zoologist

You know, lady and gentlemans, I got a frien' w'at wen' college. Now it's a school in Taxes an' I don' tole you where 'cause I don' wan' to reflact no college nowhere. I wen' to L.U.S. five year an' I would still be a frashman if I wen' back. So I'm not gon' talk 'bout any college. He brought hisse'f to dis college an' he study dat stuff how-you-call zoology. You know, bugs, snakes, take a crawfish all apart an' don't eat it—dat's sacrilege.

An' one day, he was conductin' a spear-a-ment. He got his white coat on an' he got a box, got tweezers—in bot' han's—an' he got a pad an' pencil to make notes on. He put dat box an' dem tweezers an' dat microscope all down, an' he get dat pad an' dat pencil an' he write somet'ing on dair real fast, den he put it down. He reach an' open dat box an' he take dem tweezers an' pick up a flea w'at he got in dair.

An' he grab dem flea an'—*creak*—he tear off one leg an' he put dat flea down an' he say, "Jomp." *Kerchoom*—dat flea jomp an' r'at now. He pick up dem pad an' pencil an' he wrote on dair.

He put dem down and reach in dat box ag'in an' get dat flea an' he tear anodder leg off an' he put dat flea down an' he say, "Jomp." An' dat flea jomp an' r'at now. He pick up dem pad wit' dem pencil an' he write summore note on dair 'bout w'at took place, you know.

He put de pad an' pencil down an' reach an' get dat flea an' he pull off dem leg an' every time he put dat flea down, he holler, "Jomp," an' *choom,* dat flea jomp an' r'at now. An' he make a note averytime on his pad wit' his pencil.

He got one leg lef' an' he reach wit' dem tweezers an' get dat flea an' he grab dat last leg an' *creak*—he pull it off. He put dat flea down an' he say, "Jomp." Well, de flea don' did not'ing. An' he pick up dem pad wit' dem pencil an' he write down dair real careful, "W'en you pull off all dem legs off dat flea, it cannot hear one damn t'ing."

Two Pants

I know a young couple w'at got married savarel year back, an' one day after dey were firs' made marriage, de husban' brought hisse'f home an' his wife met him at de do' jus' cryin', *whoo!* Her heart had done broke isse'f. He say, "Darlin', w'at in de worl' de matter wit' you?"

She say, "Oh, I was ironin' you' bran' new suit and oh, I burned a hole all the way plum' t'rough dair."

He say, "Don' let dat make some worry on you like dat. You know dat suit got two pair o' pants."

She say, "Oh yeah, I know. I used de odder pair to patch dis pair."

The Abbeville Ace

Now I wanna tole you 'bout dis time I got a frien' w'at was rich, *whoo,* he was rich. He got a oil well dat can pump mo' oil den he can spen' de nex' day, I ga-ron-tee.

An' he got averyt'ing in de worl' he can use, an' one day he was down listenin' to all dem smaht peoples in town, in Abbeville, in de pool hall, an' he hear 'em talk 'bout dem arrow-planes an' flyin', an' he say, "I bleeve I'm gon' get one o' dat."

An' a frien' tol' him, "Look, ma' frien', you don' know how to fly one o' dem t'ings."

He say, "Dat's r'at, but I can learn."

His frien' say, "Dey don' got no place in Abbeville where you can learn."

He say, "I'll go to New Or-lee-anh to de arrow-port down dair an' learn mase'f how to fly."

De frien' say, "You ain't gon' be able to taught you'se'f, now don' start dat foolishment."

He say, "Hokay, den I'll get someone else to taught me."

So he wen' down to New Or-lee-anh and he hire a man to taught him how to fly an' it not long befo' he t'ought he Eddie Rickenbacker an' good. He t'ought he de vary bes'. He say, "Well, I'm goin' off an' make a non-stop flit from New Or-lee-anh to LaGuardia Fiel' in New York City."

Well, a fallow tole him, "Look, ma' frien', dat li'l ol' plane you got won' make a non-stop flit, not from New Or-lee-anh to LaGuardia Fiel'. You gon' have to stop an' get you'se'f some gasoline on dat flit." He say, "I can did dat."

So he made a non-stop flit to Montgomery, Alabama. He turned dair an' make a non-stop flit to Nort' Atlanta, Georgia. He non-stop flit from dair r'at to Charlotte, Nort' Carolina. Den he non-stop flit from dair to Richmond, Virginia, an' he fulled up wit' dem gas avery time. Den he made a non-stop flit to Washington, D. an' C.

He got into dat las' leg of dat non-stop flit f'om New Or-lee-anh to LaGuardia Fiel'. He head toward LaGuardia Field an' I wan' to tol' you he got into a storm, *whoo*. Dat fog so t'ick you don' dare took a deep breathe, 'cause if you do you gon' drown you'se'f, you know. De only way in de worl' he can see his han' is to rub it on his face. Dat's how bad dat fog is.

Well, he know he gettin' close to LaGuardia Fiel' an' he notice de gasoline, dair's not too much lef'. So he pick up dem how-you-call ray-dio an' he say, "Hello, LaGuardia Field, dis is de ace number one from Abbeville, Lewisana, w'at's callin' you. Would you please give me some directions so I can find out where you at, hanh?"

LaGuardia Fiel' didn't say not'ing.

He circle aroun' an' see if he can fine jus' a li'l hole he can see t'rough. Jus' big enuf to get through is a'r'at wit' him. He circle aroun' a li'l mo' an' he notice his gas gettin' lower an' he grab dat microphone on dat ray-dio an' he say, "LaGuardia Fiel', dis is ace number one, dat's true, from Abbeville, Lewisana. But dat don' make some difference how good you are. You run out o' gas, you can' fly. An' I 'mos' out o' gas. Please, will you call me. Say hello, anyt'ing, iss hokay wit' me."

LaGuardia Fiel' didn't say a word.

He look aroun' for a hole jus' big enuf to see t'rough. Dat be a'r'at wit' him. He don' fine not'ing an' 'bout dat time, dat ol' motor go *putta putta putta, putta putt putt* . . . an' it don' go summore.

He pick up dat ray-dio an' he say, "Look, LaGuardia Fiel', dis is de ace number one from Abbeville, Lewisana, an' de time for foolishment is done pas'. I'm all de way plum' out o' gas. I ain't got some any a-tall an' it's quiet up here, I ga-ron-tee. Please, will you give me some instructions on how to fine out where you are, hanh?"

He is at ten t'ousan' feet and he go 'roun' an' 'roun' tryin' to fine a li'l bitty hole. Den he at five t'ousan' feet an' he say, "Hello, LaGuardia Fiel', I'm at five t'ousan' feet an' I need to fine out where you are, an' r'at now. Swore at me, cuss me out, tell me hello, anyt'ing, jus' so you said somet'ing wit' me."

LaGuardia Fiel' did not answer him.

He say, "LaGuardia Fiel', I'm at one t'ousan' feet. Please give me some instructions r'at now. I mean fas', fas', fas'. Dis is ace number one. LaGuardia, say somet'ing."

Dis voice come in an' say, "Ace number one, from Abbeville?"

He say, "Dass me, man, I ga-ron-tee. You got de r'at one! W'at's you' instruction? He'p me, LaGuardia Fiel', he'p me. W'at's you' instruction an' r'at now?"

De voice say, "Dis is LaGuardia Fiel'. Repeat after us: now I lay me down to sleep. . ."

Challenging the Jury

I walked in de cou'thouse in Livingston not long ago where I am a deputy sheriff. I wen' to see de chief deputy an' dey say, "He's in de cou'troom. Dey tryin' a new case in dair."

I walked in dair an' dis fallow mus' have done somet'ing real bad 'cause dey had twelve peoples in de jury, you know. Jus' as I walk in, de judge ax dat defendin' lawyer people, "Ax you' clien' if he would like to challenge de jury."

De fallow say, "Would you like to challenge de jury?"

Dat accuse' fallow stan' hisse'f up an' he look dat jury up one side an' down de same side den back up de odder side summore. He say, "I'll take on dat li'l bitty son-o'-a-gun sittin' on de end r'at down dair."

The Canine Bourré Player

For many year down in French Settlement, dair was a bourré game—dass Cajun poker, only a lot quicker—dat wen' on fo' twenty-fo' hour a day fo' over twenty year dat I know 'bout. I know; I been in it. An' in de li'l bar where it took place, it ran all de time an' de bartender would took de place o' someone so someone could go work an' make a li'l money an' come back an' play bourré.

An' de game would never have over six peoples an' never unner t'ree, to keep de game goin'. Well, one day dey was havin' a game an' de bartender was playin a'ready. An' you walk in dair to get a drink an' he playin, jus' sit down an' wait 'cause he ain't gon' leave de table 'til he can deal in wit' somet'ing.

Dey got dis game goin' real good an' one o' dem Cajuns playin' say, "Look, I ain't been to bed in t'irty-t'ree hour an' I'm sleepy like hell. An' you playin' a'ready an' I don' know w'at I'm gon' did. But I'm jus' so tired I'm look at fo' card all de time an' I ain't got but one. But I got to res'. I know w'at I'm gon' did."

An' he call his dog Phideaux. He say, "Phideaux, jomp up here an' play ma' han' so I can res' mase'f." Well, ol' Phideaux jomp up dair an' he play his han'.

Well, a city-slickin' fallow walk in dair an' he see dat dog playin' bourré an' he don' said not'ing. After a while, he say, "Dat's de smartes' dog I never see befo' ag'in in ma' life. *Whooo.* Whose dog dat is?"

Dat Cajun wake up an' say, "Dat's ma' dog. Let him alone."

He say, "Oh, I ain't gon' bodder him. I tell you r'at now. Dat dog should be in a sideshow or in a circus or someplace, 'cause he is de vary smartes' dog in de worl'."

Dat Cajun say, "I don' t'ink he so damn smart."

De city fallow say, "W'at make you say somet'ing like dat?"

De Cajun say, "Look at him. Every time he got a good han', he wag his tail, I ga-ron-tee!"

The Truthful Sheriff's Dog

I got a good frien' name Gordon Martin an' he is the sheriff of St. James Parish. St. James Parish is between Bat-onh Rouge an' New Or-lee-anh on the Mississippi River. De river cut it in two, in fac'. Now Gordon been sheriff down dair a long time, twenty-fo' year, an' he a fine man. He really is. He done a fine job as sheriff an' he's a concrete axample dat we do still have hones' politicians.

Not long ago, Sheriff Martin was sittin' in de cou'thouse dair in

Convent, Lewisana, sittin' dair in one o' dem captain's chairs (even t'ough he de sheriff) an' down on de flo' by de side o' him is a great big lickin' pot houn', a Lewisana Catahoula dog. Dey call it leopard dog in Taxes, not knowin' no better. An' dey born mean, you got to taught 'em how to be good.

An' Sheriff Martin jus' shakin' han's wit' all his constitoots w'at come by dair, you know. He's runnin' ag'in. An' a fallow come in dair all dress up, coat an' tie. You can tell he work fo' de governmen', don' do too damn much. He say, "Hi, Sheriff, I'm glad fo' you to see me." Sheriff Martin say, "I'm glad fo' you to see me, too. How de fam'ly?" "Oh," he say, "dey jus' fine."

De fallow say, "Sheriff, does you' dog bite, hanh?"

Sheriff Martin say, "You know de sheriff couldn't have a dog w'at bite." Dat fallow reach down to pet dat dog, an' *younk,* he 'mos' bit his han' off!

Well, dey rush 'roun' dair an' give him firs' aid—OSHA made dem learn how to did dat—an' wrap his han' all up good. He say, "Sheriff, I t'ought you tole me you' dog don' bite."

Sheriff Martin say, "Ma' dog don' bite."

He say, "De hell he don'. Look at ma' han'."

Sheriff Martin say, "Dat ain't ma' dog."

Four Duck Hunters

I got fo' frien's an' dey wen' hontin' down near Sabine Pass on de Lewisana side 'bout two year ago an' dock were averywhere. Dair's fo' o' dem—I'm talk 'bout peoples, not dock—an' dey shot dem dock 'til dey guns got hot.

Dey didn't have no Lab'ador retriever wit' dem, so dey jus' let de dock fall an' de wind push 'em up ag'inst de reeds. Well, dey finally run out o' shell an' dey say, "We got to go to de house. Less get our dock an' go."

Dey start out and dair's two great big game wardens standin' dair an' dey say, "Wait jus' a minnit an' we'll pick up you' dock fo' you."

So dey count dem dock, an' dis a true story, lady an' gentlemans, 250 dock. De head game warden look at dem sittin' dair, two in one pirogue boat an' two in de odder. He look at dat firs' one an' he say, "How many dock did you get?" "Oh," he say, "I got ma' limit."

He look at de secon' one. "How many dock did you get?" He say, "Oh, me, I got ma' limit, too."

He ax dat t'ird one, "How 'bout you?" He say, "I ga-ron-tee I got ma' limit."

W'en he get to dat fo'rt' one, he say, "Well, how many dock did you get?"

He say, "I guess de res' o' dem is mine."

The Cajun Hunter

I got to tole you dis story 'bout goin' squirrel hontin' w'at a Cajun tole me to be de trut'. You can doubt ma' word even t'ough I am a defender o' de trut'. I didn't say I said it, but I'll defend de hell out o' it. But I bleeve dis Cajun.

Dair was a fallow las' squirrel season—we got a lot o' squirrel down dair where I live—an' he wen' out dair de firs' day an' he didn't ree-lize dat peoples had done been in dair an' got mos' of dem squirrel. But de wood is dry, *whoo* iss dry. An' he make enuf noise soun' like one o' dem caterpillin' tractors comin' t'rough dair wit' a bush-hog attach to de rearen' o' it. An' he jus' 'bout to los' his discourage 'cause he ain't seen a live squirrel at all. He done shot out some nests in de trees t'inkin' he might fine one sleepin'. But it midday an' dair ain't no squirrel sleepin'. Somebody alse done got 'em anyhow.

He jus' 'bout los' his discourage an' he run upon a li'l boy 'bout thirteen or twelve year ol' an' dat li'l boy got squirrel, *whooee.*

W'at he did, he pull de head up t'rough his belt an' let de tail hang down an' he got squirrel all de way aroun' him. Look like a hula skirt he got so many squirrel.

Dis Cajun say, "W'at you got dair?"

De li'l boy say, "W'at you t'ought I got dair? I got squirrel. Fo'teen squirrel."

He say, "Who kill 'em?"

De li'l boy say, "I kill 'em, Mister."

Now he notice dat de li'l boy ain't got no shootgun, no rifle, not even a bow an' arrow. He say, "Son, I ain't one o' dem ol' game warden. If you got a frien' over sixteen back in dem wood killin' dem squirrel, call him out. I ain't gon' said not'ing. It's a'r'at wit' me. Shucks, I'm jus' proud to see somebody gettin' dem squirrel like dat, I ga-ron-tee."

He say, "Mister, I ain't got no frien' an' I kill dem squirrel mase'f."

He say, "W'at you kill 'em wit'? A rock?"

He say, "Hell no." An' he reach in his pock-ett an' he pull a steel ball out, one inch in diameter bot' ways. He say, "I kill 'em wit' dat steel ball."

Ma' frien' say, "Look, I ain't know you t'ree minnits an' you done tole me t'ree lies. Don' you know you goin' to hell on a bobsled? Lyin' to somebody older den you like dat. You should be 'shamed you'se'f, I ga-ron-tee. I'm 'shame' wit' you."

He say, "Mister, I ain't lyin', I ga-ron-tee."

He say, "Don' garontee you' lies! Dass bad!"

He say, "But I'm not lyin', Mister. I kill dem squirrel wit' dis steel ball—SHHHH! Be quiet. Dair's a squirrel on dat lim' r'at up dair."

Well, ma' frien' shut his big mout' an' look up dair. Dair's a squirrel up dair—firs' live squirrel he see dat day. Dat li'l boy jus' flick dat lef' han' wit' dat steel ball—*choom*—knock dat squirrel out. He wen' over dair an' pick him up an' *blap, blap, blap,* beat him ag'inst de tree to make sho' he dead. Den he take off bot' shoes an' begin to feel aroun' for his steel ball in de leaves. Finally he foun' it an' he reach down an' pick it up an' put it back in his lef' han' an' put it back in his pock-ett, den put dat squirrel t'rough his belt.

Ma' frien' say, "Well, I done see averyt'ing now, but it ain't no use. Nobody gon' bleeve a damn word. Here you are, a li'l bitty ol' lef'-han' boy, chunk up dair an' knock dat squirrel out de firs' time you chunk. Me, I'm lef'-han' an' I could t'row up dair a t'ousan' time an' I wouldn't move a hair. I wouldn't move a fedder on dat squirrel."

Dat li'l boy say, "Mister, I ain't lef'-han'."

Ma' frien' say, "Don' you start dat foolishment wit' me. I jus' saw you t'row up dair lef'-han'. Don' you start dat."

De boy say, "I ain't lef'-han', Mister, I'm r'at-han'."

Ma' frien' say, "How come you did not t'row up dair r'at-han', hanh?"

De li'l boy say, "Papa won't let me."

Ma' frien' say, "How come you' papa won't let you chunk r'at-han'?"

Dat boy say, "I tear 'em up too bad."

The High-Jumping Bear Hunter

You know, in de Atchafalaya River swamp an' spillway, we still got some o' dem li'l black bear. Dey ain't so damn li'l at dat. Anyt'ing weigh 300 pound ain't so li'l, no. An' I got a frien' w'at wen' down in dat swamp 'cause he wanted to got one o' dem bear rug fo' de flo'.

He say, "I wen' down dair, me, an' I look an' I look an' pass ma' eyeball ag'in—not'ing a-tall. I was so tired w'en I came to dis big open space, mus' be 100 acres. I spy jus' one tree r'at in de middle. Dair's jus' one branch on dat tree, r'at in de middle an' twenty-two foots, one inch from de groun'. Since I didn't find no bears, me, I t'ought I'd took a li'l snooze r'at dair. An' I took ma' twice-barrel Caribbean (dass a two-hole gun), stood it up, an' I fell asleep.

"When I'm woke up, one dem li'l black bear done fine me, an' I'm woke an' gone wit' de same breeze—*choom!* I'm headed fo' de tree wit' de li'l black bear t'ree step behin' tryin' to make it two.

"I'm headed fo' de tree wit' de black bear breathin' down ma' neck r'at wit' his mout' wide open, look like he laffin' at somet'ing. I got to de tree an' I jumped fo' de limb swinging."

I say, "Did you caught dat limb, hanh?"

"I miss it on de way up," he say, "but I caught it on de way down, I ga-ron-tee!"

Preposterous Possum

I got a frien' name Murphy Brown fishes all de time—loves to catch dem turtle, snapper an' loggerhead. Some year ago, Brown ax me if I could fine him someplace to hont dem deer in Taxes. "Sure, I know some peoples in Houston, Taxes, will took you deer hontin'," I said. So I called dese peoples in Houston, Taxes, an' dey said, "Sure, bring Murphy out cheer an' we'll pass a good time wit' him."

So I sent Murphy on out dair, an' in de camp dey showed him some comforts an' pleasures of de hont firs-class. Dey had heated blin's an' feed throwers where you can coax dem deer closer befo' shootin' 'em.

Murphy got hisse'f up early next mornin', an' he was so impatient to get gone dey tole him, "Look, you don' got to wait fo' us, no. Jus' took dis road an' turn to de lef' 'bout a mile, an' anodder lef' an' you gon' fine de deer camp r'at dair. Stay dair as long as you like, an' if you ain't ready by night, we'll come get you. If you got ready earlier, jus' walk you'se'f back de same way you came."

W'en he didn't show up by suppertime, dey sent a guide fo' him. De camp was deserted, but nearby dey foun' a pool o' blood, an' dey traced it back to de compound. To dey immense relief, dey foun' Murphy skinnin' a armadillo.

"You know," said Murphy, "dis is de firs' hard-shell possum I never see befo' ag'in in ma' life."

Sure Cure for a Sick Mule

Not long ago, I was down in Johnny Guitreau's run by ma' good frien' Peggy Bercegeay—an' dat's de place where you can go any mornin' at quarter to five (I'm talk 'bout 4:45 a.m. in de mornin') an' sit at de bar wit' a whole new bunch to get dronk wit' if you wan' to, dey dair. You go back at ten o'clock an' dey still dair, too. An' at ten o'clock, you can ax one o' dem, you say, "How 'bout a beer?" He say, "I might try one."

Well, I was in dair one day jus' a few week ago talkin' wit' a frien' wit' me, an' anodder Cajun come in dair an' he walk up to dis Cajun w'at I'm talk wit' an' he say, "Hey, ma' frien', you maybe can he'p me. Ma' ol' mule w'at I got to make ma' garden wit' an' is hard to get now is sick like hell. I don' know w'at wrong wit' him. He got de corlic or somet'ing. I don' know. Maybe even worm. I don' know. Maybe you can tell me w'at I can did."

Ma' frien' say, "Ma' ol' mule got sick like dat an' I gave him a quart o' turpentine."

Well, de farmer say, "T'ank you," an' he lef'. He wen' by de hardware sto', pick up a quart o' turpentine, wen' home, gave it to de ol' mule, an' kill him deader den hell.

An' 'bout fo' or t'ree day later, he was back in Johnny Guitreau's an' I happen to be dair summore, drinkin' buttermilk, an' he walk to dis same Cajun an' he say, "Hey, didn't you tole me you gave you' mule a quart o' turpentine?"

He say, "Dass r'at."

He say, "Well, I gave ma' mule a quart o' turpentine an' it kill him deader den hell."

De firs' one say, "Kill mine, too."

A Young Fish Thief

I got a good frien' dat live down dair in Gonzales an' he got a nice store an' fish market. He's one o' de kindes'-heart peoples I ever knew. Iss a wonder he been able to make a livin', but he has 'cause peoples, bleeve it or not, haven't taken advantage o' him 'cause he's so good.

At dis fish market dair he had a hard time keepin' help, an' he haul off an' hire a young fallow. He was pore. He felt pore. He look pore. In fac', he couldn't sweat, 'cause I never saw a bone sweat.

An' he went to work for dis man, an' he work hard. He start pickin' up a li'l weight an' lookin' better. An' ma' frien' love him—he work so good. But ma' frien' also knew too dat he miss a fish avery night, an' dat fallow was de one takin' him home under his coat.

Ma' frien' got a problem; he don' wan' to fire de pore fallow. He finally make a decide to warn de worker in a nice way. He say, "I wan' you to did me a favor. Now, either got you'se'f a longer coat, or start stealin' shorter fish."

Shoe Repair

I got a frien' live in Thibodaux who fish wit' me all de time. He loves to fish almos' as much as me. Only trouble, he got to work mos' o' de week while I work on de weekends, so we don' got much time to be toget'er—'cept now an' den avery once in a while.

His wife is a cur-ous lady, like mos' us Cajuns. She tole him, "Look, you know somet'ing? You got to clean out de h'attic o' dem house up dair, 'cause if you don' did dat, it'll happen like dem odder fires aroun' here start in de h'attic."

She kept on fo' six week an' interfere wit' his fishin' bad. But finally he couldn't stood dat no more. One Sattiday mornin', he say, "You know w'at I'm gon' did?" She say, "Go fishin'?" He say, "No, I'm gon' clean up dat h'attic, me." "Well, good fo' you," she said.

So he start cleanin' de h'attic, t'rowin' stuff r'at an' lef'.

Suddenly avert'ing got quiet up dair, an' his wife holler, "W'at de matter up dair?"

He say, "Guess w'at I foun'. I foun' a claim check for a pair of shoes. I lef' dem up dair twenty year ago. I jus' wonder if dey still got 'em."

She say, "Less go see."

Dey get in dat auromobile quick, quick, quick, go to de shoemaker's in Gonzales, go to de shoe shop, put dat claim check on de counter. Ma' frien' say, "You got ma' shoe, hanh?"

De shoemaker say, "Wait here an' I'll go see."

He comes back wit', "Were dose brown low-quarters?"

"Dass r'at."

"You wanted a hole sewn in de heel?"

"Hell yeah."

De shoemaker say, "Dey'll be ready Tuesday. Don' rush me!"

The Unenlightened Swimmer

Savarel year ago dair was a beautimous young lady who lived near me in French Settlement, an' she got a job wit' de Silver Service in Dallas, Taxes. She had to took a six-mont' trainin' cou'se. Soon she met a boy an' fell plum' flat in love all de way wit' him. Dey cou't up a storm an' she fo'got to go home fo' fo' year. But dey had dair firs' fuss, an' she say, "Me, I'm goin' to see Mama."

Well, she wen' back home in French Settlement, an' she was glad to got back an' see dem lovely trees an' dat magnifique water in de bayou. De water look so invitin' one day dat she went in wit' her birt'day suits on. But w'en she got out an' went to fetch her clothes, dey had disappear. "Somebody done stole ma clothes. W'at I'm gon' did now?" she wailed.

'Bout dat time she hear somebody whistlin' cheerful-like an' comin' in her direction, an' she look to see a young fallow comin' wit' a string of fish. She suspec' he might be de clothes t'ief, an' as he came closer she found a discard dispan an' quickly put it in fron' o' her. "Dat's de fallow, dat's de t'ief," she repeat to herse'f. "He expec' to see me in ma' birt'day suits, but I'm gon' fool him, me."

W'en he got closer, she say, "You wanna know w'at I t'ink?"

He say, "I know w'at you t'ink. You t'ink dat dat dishpan got a bottom in it, but I know better!"

Last Rites for a Feline Companion

I had a frien' dat live down in Lafourche Parish, near Thibodaux, an' he had a boat—one dem sea-goin' job. Well, he haul off an' drop dead f'om w'at dey call high-pretension. Dat made his wife a female lady widow womans. Dey got no spring-off, an' dey rich like hell. Even got oil well an' t'ings like dat.

But de only t'ing dis woman female lady got dat she love was a beautimous white Persian cat. She shower infection on dis cat all de time.

One day de cat drop isse'f dead—all nine lives at one time. It mos' broke her heart into a million litter-bitty pieces. She say, "Me, I'm gon' give dat cat a good funeral—de vary bes'."

She had a bronze casket made, an' she put some satin an' silk in dair, an' den wen' to see de pries'.

"Fat'er," she say, "will you bury my cat fo' me, hanh?"

"W'at you said?"

"Will you bury my cat fo' me?"

"I can't did dat. Cats are animules, not peoples, no."

"Well," she say, "I got $25,000 to bury him wit'. Maybe de Baptis' minister will perform de nuptial."

"Hol' you'se'f still an' brought you'se'f back," de pries' say. "You didn't tole me dat cat was Cat-lic."

Smart Barber

I got a frien' w'at hit it rich an' sol' five t'ousan' acre of lan' for $500 'piece, an' he was sittin' nex' to me in de barber cheer. He say to de barber like dis, "Me, I'm gon' took de ol' lady to Rome. We gon' stay at de Excelsior Hotel dair, an' we gon' got us a audience wit' de Pope." An' de barber, who got to mess in averybody alse business, say, "You don' want to did dat. W'at arrow-line you gon' go, hanh?"

"National," ma' frien' say.

"Dass a big mistook," de barber say. "Dat National Arrow-line got all ol' equipmen', an' de stewardess are de oldes' peoples dey got workin' fo' dem. Where you gonna stay?"

"At de Excelsior Hotel."

"Don' did dat," de barberin' man say. "Dey ain't got no room service dair, de furniture is ol' an' broken-down, an' de bedspring so bad it likely to stab you in de back f'om a broke spring. As for de Pope, he'll see you wit' fifty-t'ousan' odders, an' you won't know who he's talkin' to. Why you go?"

"I got to go," de man say. "Ma' wife insis' I do."

Well, 'bout eight week pass an' de man come back in to de barber shop an' got in de cheer. "Well, did you go to Italy?" de barber say.

"You ain't jus' a whistlin' Big Mamou," ma' frien' say. "An' you wrong 'bout dat National Arrow-line. Dey had all new equipmen', an' de stewardess so nice ma' wife won't let me unbuckle ma' seat belt all de way. An' de Excelsior Hotel got averyt'ing new an' de service is perfec'."

"An' de Pope?"

"You wrong about dat, too. Me an' ma' wife wit' anodder couple speak wit' him for half a hour, an' I want you to know he speak good English, like me. Den we stoop down to receive de how-you-call papal blessin' an' he put his han' on de odder couple's head, an' den ma' wife, an' den me. W'en he got to me, he say, 'Where you got dat terrible hairscut? You better go to anodder barber, you.' "

Fishin' Game Warden

I got a frien' live down in Port Vincent, fishin' down dair all de time. An' avery time he got hisse'f back to lan' where dey launch dem boat, he got a boatload o' fish—all kinds o' fish—buffalo, big mout' basses, li'l mout' basses, goggle-eye perch, bream, eel, sometimes alligator. One day de game warden say, "Man, you caught some fish."

"You damn r'at," de li'l fisherman say.

"I would like to go wit' you sometimes," say de warden.

"I'd be glad to took you along," dat Cajun say, "but you got to brought you'se'f here befo' t'ree o'clock in de mornin'."

Nex' mornin' early de game warden was dair an' dey got inside dat boat. It was dark, I mean! Jus' like de insides o' a cow. Only way you could see you' hand was to rub it hard on you' face.

Dey started down dat Amite River jus' at de dawn, an' soon de li'l Cajun stopped de motor an' cast anchor. De game warden touch him on de shoulder an' say, "Hey, man, you better pull up anchor. You lef' all you' fishin' tackle back at de dock. We gotta go back dair an' start over."

De li'l Cajun don' say a word. He reach under dat seat an' got a brown box, one feets long an' one-ha'f feets deep. He open it up, reach in, an' got a stick o' dynamite. He stuck a cap in it, lit de sho't fuse wit' his seegar, den chuck de dynamite into de river. *Bloom!* Fish averywhere.

De game warden jus' sit dair wit' his mout' wide open, like he was catchin' a fly. After he got his spoke back, he sputter, "Hey man, don' you know dat's ag'inst de law? Don' you know dat's illegal as hell? Don' you ree-lize I'm de game warden gotta put you in jail?"

De li'l Cajun don' said a word. Open dat box up, got anodder stick o' dynamite, got anodder cap. Stuck it in dair, got a sho't fuse, clamped it down wit' his teet', lit de fuse wit' his seegar, stuck dat stick o' dynamite in de game warden's han' an' say, "Look, you gon' talk or fish?"

Police Radio Dispatcher

I have a police radio in ma' car, an' de odder day I was goin' down de road w'en I heard dis dispatcher f'om somewhere in de Teche country call, "Dis is kick-ee t'ree t' saven t'ree. Callin' car number one."

An' car number one say, "Go 'head wit' you' message."

"W'at you' 10-20?"

"I'm 10-4 on you. I'm on de interstate headin' eas'."

"Well, I called to let you know dair's a dead horse headin' wes' on de interstate."

The Diplomat

I got t'ree frien's in Livingston Parish. One live in French Settlement, one live in Maurepas, an' one live in Frost. An' dese t'ree community form a triangle—no matter how you look at it, dere's still nine mile between 'em. An' dese t'ree frien's wit' me been working in construction toget'er for fifteen or fo'teen year, but dey fam'ly don' know each odder some a-tall any, an' how come de reason is 'cause dey got a school in each one o' dese community an' iss still de community center. We don' got a busing problem down here; we don' got no buses.

Dese t'ree men, dey meet at de Y. Dat's right nort' of French Settlement where the Moonlight Inn is on one side an' Brignac's Stompin' Place used to be on de odder 'till somebody set it on fire dancin' too fas'. Dey meet dair in dey country Cadillac (dass a pickin'-up truck), dey leave two o' dem truck dair, an' dey go to work in one an' dey rotation dat aroun' so dey don' wear none o' dem out too fas'.

One Friday dey got paid, an' on de way home dey stopped at a barroom saloon cocktail loonge. Dey drink a lot o' dat good Cajun whiskey made up in Tennessee, Jacques Dan-yell, an' chase it wit' pop wit' foam on top, an' dey fall dronk. In fac', one o' dem get too dronk to sing so he got to drive. An' he was drivin' dat country Cadillac along, de road turn, he don', an' *blap!* Up ag'ins' one o' dem lovely live oak trees dat John McKeithen missed when he was governor. He totalated dat truck all de way, plum'. Two o' dem don' get a scratchin' on dem, but de t'ird one, pore ol' Boudreaux, is dead.

One say, "W'at we gon' did, hanh?"

"W'atchoo mean, 'W'at we gon' did'? He's dead, we can't do not'ing."

"Oh, no, we got to call de state police an' de coroner. You can't lef' him in a ditch, he got to go to de fun'ral home. Dat ain't all. Somebody got to tell his wife. You know Mrs. Boudreaux?"

"Hell no. An' I can't take good news, let alone bad news."

He say, "You call de state police an' de sheriff an' de coroner an' see dat Boudreaux goes somewhere. I am broke out wit' tack. In fack, I ought to be a diplomacer, I got so much tack."

He say, "Took you' tack an' go tole her."

He took his tack an' he lef'. He went to Boudreaux's house in French Settlement. *Flap, flap, flap,* on de do'. Dis lady brought herself to de do' an' he look up at her an' say, "Are you de widder Boudreaux?"

"I'm Mrs. Boudreaux, me," say de lady, "but I ain't no widder."

He say, "De hell you ain't."

An Honest Driver

Years ago I lived in Crowley, Lewisana, an' dair was a ol' Cajun who had a bakery down dair. He was one o' de leadin' citizens down dair. An' avery day, he would back his car out o' de bakery an' go home.

Well, one day he back his Cadillac out an' get to de red light an' *shoom.* He run dat red light. Dair was a policeman on de corner dair, an' he blew his whistle an' stop him.

He been on de corner for years an' he knew de ol' man an' he didn't wan' to give him a ticket, no. So he call him by name an' he say, "Did you not see dat red light, hanh?"

De ol' man say, "Hell yeah. But I did not see you, I ga-ron-tee!"

Inquiring Optometrist

I was in Jerry Henderson's—ma' optometrist's—office one day an' dis Cajun come in dair an' he say, "Hey, Doc. I can't see as good as I used to. Mus' be ma' eyes, hanh?"

Ol' Jerry, vary professional-like, say, "It could be. Come in year an' less us fill out dis form on you."

"Oh, we gon' fill out a form?"

"Oh, iss jus' a matter o' practice. Now, w'at you' name?" He tole him an' Jerry wrote it down.

"How ol' you are?"

"You got to know dat, Doc?"

Jerry say, "I wouldn' ax it if I didn't have to know." So de Cajun tole him.

Den Jerry say, "Where you live?"

Dat Cajun say, "You comin' to see me, Doc?"

Jerry say, "We got to know where to sen' de bill." He say, "Hokay," an' tole him where to sen' de bill.

Jerry look at him an' say, "Now I wan' to ax you. Have you' eyes ever been scheck?"

He say, "Hell no, Doc. Dey always been blue."

Frugal Husband

De odder day I was at ma' dentis', an' I was up in dat cheer an' he had ma' mout' full of dat grit, you know w'at I mean. An' a Cajun jus' bust in his office. "Hey, Doc!"

De doc say, "Can't you see I'm busy?"

"Oh, hell yeah. Go 'head on. I jus' wan' ax you somet'ing." He say, "How much you charge to put dem gases on somebody an' pull dem teet'?"

De doc say, "How many teet'?"

He say, "One teet'."

De doc say, "Saventy-five dollar."

"Saventy-five dollar?"

"Dat's r'at, saventy-five dollar."

"Well, how much you charge jus' to put dem needle down dair an' dead dat gum a li'l bit an' den pull dem teet'?"

"Fifteen dollar."

"Fifteen dollar?"

"Dass r'at."

Dat Cajun say, "Doc, how much you charge jus' to reach in dair wit' dose pliers an' get dat teet' CREEK, wit' no gases or no needles?"

De doc say, "Five dollar."

De Cajun talk wit' hisse'f. "Saventy-five dollar to put dem gases, fifteen dollar to use dem needle, five dollar—Doc, you sure you get all dat teet'?"

"Hell yeah, I'll get all dat teet'."

"Ma-ma, step up in dat cheer an' r'at now."

Keen-Eyed Witness

Not long ago in court at Livingston, dey had a witness on de stan', a Cajun boy from down dair in de parish. Dey were tryin' a man fo' aggravated insult. In Lewisana dat means you use a knife or tire tool or a gun or brass knucks—somet'ing mo' den you' bare fis'.

Dis Cajun was on de stan' an' de defense lawyer said to de witness, "I unnerstan' you witness dis altercation."

He say, "I didn't do dat, but I saw a damn good fight."

"Dass w'at I'm talk about. Now you saw dis . . ."

"Oh, hell yeah."

De judge interrupt, "Confine you'se'f to de question."

De lawyer say, "Now would you min' describe de accuse'?"
De witness say, "Oh, he sittin' r'at over dair."
"I know, but can you describe w'at he was wearin'?"
"Well, a brown suits wit' little yellow pinstripes, an' he had on green socks wit' yellow clock on de ankle. Had on one o' dem li'l hats call houn's-toot' like Bear Bryant in Alabama University got. Had on a wris'watch wit' a ludicous dial. He had a knife—big knife."
De lawyer say, "How far were you f'om dis fight, hanh?"
" 'Bout six block."
"You mean to tole me you were six block away an' saw all dat?"
"Oh, hell yeah." "You can see damn good, can't you?" "Oh, hell yeah. I can see de moon damn good, an' it 260,000 mile."

Sheriff's Dispatcher

W'en I'm home in Livingston Parish, I'm a deputy sheriff on call 24 hours a day, an' I always call in to see w'at been goin' on. Not 'cause I'm a good deputy sheriff, but 'cause I got a big cur-ous.
An' we got a dispatcher dair, fine young man, really an' truly, deserves a lot o' credit, an' his name is Johnny Sanders. An' I always call him an' ax Johnny w'at been goin' on an' he always tell me.
An' a year or so ago, I got in. I been on a long speakin' tour, ma' maximum time nine days to be away from Sout' Lewisana. An' I call him an' I say, "How you doin'?" He say, "Jus' fine, Juice-tanh." I say, "W'at been goin' on?"
He say, "We been busy like hell."
I say, "You don' mean to tole me."
Well, he name a fallow. "Got shot," he say.
I say, "He did? Bad?"
"Hell yeah," he say, "t'rough an' t'rough de head."
"Oh," I say, "killed him, hanh?"
He say, "No, but he'll never be de same, I ga-ron-tee."

Innovative Chicken Farmer

You know, I can't he'p but remember w'en Travis Lobell start dat schicken farm. He didn't have but a hunnert schickens an' he an' his wife Jeannie were raisin' dem schickens an' gettin' dem aggs, but he live r'at on a highway an' *shoom, shoom, shoom, shoom,* dem peoples go by dair an' kill dem schickens as fas' as he could get 'em up big enuf to lay aggs, you know.

So he start callin' de state police. "You got to did somet'ing 'bout dese drivers drivin' so fas' an' killin' all my schickens." Well, de state police was jus' doin' dere bes' to he'p, so dey came out dair an' put up a big sign, Slow, Plant Entrance. *Shoom, shoom, shoom, shoom,* look like it speed 'em up.

An' ol' Travis call 'em every day, at leas' ten time a day. "You got to did somet'ing. Dat 'plant entrance' sign did not did some good, some a-tall any." Well, dey say, "Hokay," an' dey come out dair an' dey sen' de highway depahtment out dair an' dey put a sign, Slow, Chirren at Play, an' dat really speed 'em up, *shoom, shoom, shoom, shoom.*

Well, he call an' he call an' he call. Finally he call up one day an' he say, "Look, Cap, do you min', is it legal fo' me to put ma' own damn sign, hanh?" De captain jus' wan' to get rid o' him so damn bad, he say, "Hell yeah. Go 'head on. Put you' sign up. Jus' do anyt'ing, any kine o' sign dat gon' slow dem peoples up." Travis say, "Hokay."

Well, dat policemans didn't hear from ol' Travis Lobell for t'irty days. An' one day he ax his lieutenant, "You heard from dat fallow Lobell?" He say, "Hell no, I ain't heard from him. You heard from him, Captain?" "No, dat's how come I ax you."

De captain ax his sergeant, "Bill, you heard from Lobell?" "Oh, hell no, Captain. T'ank goodness." "Well, I ain't heard f'om him in t'irty days, so I guess I better call him up an' see w'at he did," de captain say.

So he call him up: "Mister Lobell, dis is Captain Walker wit' de state police."

"Well, hello dair, Cap. How you are? I jus' want to let you know, Cap, dat I put a sign up dat slow dem devils down. I ain't got a schicken kill in t'irty days."

Captain Walker say, "You don' mean to tole me."

Travis say, "Dat's r'at. T'ank you, Cap, I'm busy. I got to go." An' he hung up.

De captain say, "We better go scheck up on dat sign. It may be somet'ing we can use in a lot o' places." So he sen' a man, he sen' Lieutenant Melancon. He drove up dair to Travis's place in Springfiel' an' dair's a great big sign, a whole piece of plywood: Slow, Nudist Colony.

Hoping for a Full Moon

I got a couple o' li'l true t'ings I wan' to tell you. Sometimes I can't he'p but t'ink 'bout Gran'ma Malbrough, bless her wonnerful heart. W'en Neil Armstrong firs' wen' to de moon, she was ninety-one, an' her son Jean-Pierre an' I wen' dair to dat nursin' home where she stay. An' Jean-Pierre say, "Look, Gran'ma, we got to leave. We got to go watch de television an' see dem men goin' to de moon. Dey gon' lan' on de moon."

An' she look at him, lady an' gentlemans, as serial as anybody can get, an' say, "Mon Dieu, I hope dat moon is full w'en dem boys try to lan' on dair."

Revenge

Now, dis li'l story is true. I don' know how many of you ever have a toot'ache in your life. I have an' I can still have 'em, I wan' you to know.

But I got a frien' w'at live down dair in Sout'eas' Lewisana savarel year ago w'en we didn't get paid much. He made a dollar a day, I t'ink, an' dat was 75 cents mo' den I was makin'. An' he got a teet' dat hurt him so bad, he don' know w'at he gon' did an' he don' got enuf money to go to dem dentis'. He work for six week an' dem damn teet' hurt him all de time. Jus' 'bout to drove him plum' crazy.

W'en he got enuf money to go to de dentis', he go an' he say, "Doc, pull dis damn t'ing an' r'at now."

De doc-taire say, "I don' know."

He say, "Don' talk 'bout it. Pull it. I can't stood it summore."

Well, de doc-taire get a pair of dem pliers, an' he get in dair, and *keroom,* he pull dat jaw teet' out o' dair w'at had hurt dat Cajun for six long week.

He say, "Doc, would you min' lettin' me took dat teet' home wit' me?"

De doc say, "No, I don' min'. You can have you' teet'." He wrap it up an' give it to him.

Dat Cajun get home an' he get a platter, a great big platter. He put dat teet' in de middle of dat platter an' he get a whole half a gallon o' syrup, dat ol' sugar cane syrup, an' he pour it on dat teet'.

He tell dat teet', "Go on an' hurt, damn you. Hurt all you wan' to."

The Graduate

Dair was a frien' o' mine who son granulated from college an' his fat'er want a pitcher wit' him in his cap an' gown an' his granulation suit.

So he got de photo-grapher an' got toget'er dair an' de photo-grapher did his lavel bes' to pose 'em up real good. You know, some peoples stay pose an' odder people don'.

So he was tryin' his lavel bes' to get dem fix jus' r'at an' he tole de young fallow, he say, "Look, young man, put you' han' on you' fat'er's shoulder dair, like dat."

His pa-pa say, "Don' you t'ink it would be a hell o' a lot more convincin' if he put his han' in ma' pock-ett?"

The Helpful Waitress

One day down dair in Sout' Lewisana, I walk mase'f into a li'l res-rant cafe, an' de cutes', pretties' li'l female woman waitress reproach ma' table an' say, "W'at can I did fo' you, hanh?"

"Brought me de blue plate spacial, you pretty li'l t'ing," I said.

W'en I finish de blue plate spacial wit'out knowin' w'at it was, I ax her like dis, "W'at you got dair fo' dessert, you pretty li'l beautimous female woman waitress, you?"

An' she say, "We got two kine apple pie, apple an' pineapple, an' we got two kine mince pie, mince an' peppermince."

"Brought me de apple pie," I ax her.

W'en she come back wit' de dessert, she say, "Mister, you a nice man, yeah. I wan' you to did me a favor."

"Anyt'ing, bêbe," I say to her. "De sky de limit."

"Well," she say, "I wan' you to beat on dat pie wit' you' fork. If a roach don' run hisse'f out, don' you eat dat pie, 'cause dat mean he still in dair."

Fishy Story

Not long ago, I got a frien' w'at wen' fishin' on one o' dem pretty river w'at we got down dair—not a bayou, no. We got bayous, but he wen' on a river.

He got one o' dem li'l stool w'at got a pock-ett unnerneat' where you can put a six-packet if you want. You could put Coca-Cola if you wan', but dis Cajun had a six-packet o' dat pop wit' foam on top.

An' de wors' t'ing dat can happen to any fisherman happen wit' him. He ran out o' bait jus' as de fish start to bite, an' dass bad, I ga-ron-tee. He say, "Look at dis." He so disgusted wit' hisse'f dat he reach in dat pock-ett an' grab one o' dem pop wit' foam on top an' he take fo' or t'ree sip.

W'en he start to put it back, he see a li'l spring frog down dair, an' he know dey make good bait for dem bream perch. (Dey are good bait for goggle-eye, also, too.) He reach for dat frog and *shoom,* dat frog gone. He reach ag'in an' anodder frog gone.

He 'bout to los' his discourage w'en he see a li'l garter snake w'at done caught one dem frog. He reach fo' dat snake an' he caught dat 'cause dat snake can't jomp, 'specially wit' dat frog in his mout'. He say, "Ma' frien', I need dat frog more den you. You'll never know jus' how much I need dat frog." An' he take de frog away from de snake.

W'en he did dat, dat li'l snake look so pitiful, he jus' can't stood it. So he reach an' get dat bottle o' pop wit' foam on top an' he pour t'ree drop in dat snake mout'. Den he put dat snake down, put de frog on his hook an' t'row him out.

Kerplop, he done got a fish an' a nice big bream perch. He say, "*Whoo boy,* now dis mo' like it." He t'row him out ag'in an' caught anodder, den anodder, an' anodder. All on de same frog bait.

'Bout dat time he feel somet'ing rub real hard ag'inst his leg. He look down, an' dat snake done brought him anodder frog.

Ladies' Foundation

Long time ago, w'en we still had depahtment sto's in Bat-onh Rouge, befo' de shoppin' centers, dair was a ol' Cajun lady caught dat ferry to Bat-onh Rouge an' she wen' in one o' dem big depahtment sto's. She wen' dair for jus' one reason an' dat was dat her foundation done wore out on her. She had to get a foundation, or how-you-call a girdle. In dose days, it was called a cor-sett.

An' she came in dair an' she wen' lookin' all over de whole damn store an' she could not fin' dem foundation. She's 'bout to give herse'f up plum', all de way, 'cause she done los' her discourage. An' a man, one of dem flo'walker (dey used to have flo'walkers in dem days, you know), he seed her stan' up dair an' look like she los', an' she los'.

Dat flo'walker man de mos' bow-leg man you never saw ag'in befo' in you' life. W'en he walk, he look like he roll a hoop. Like he got a tire goin' aroun', you know. He look like he on a ocean-goin' vessel, like two bicycle goin' toget'er at de same time.

Well, he walk up dair an' he say, "Lady, can I he'p you, hanh?"

An' she embarrass, *whoo,* ol' Cajun lady like dat an' she embarrass like hell. She say, "Could you tole me where de foundation garment is, hanh?"

He say, "Of cou'se." An' he turn aroun' and he say, "Walk dis way."

She say, "If I got to walk dat way, I don' wan' one o' dem damn t'ings."

Thin Slices

Dey tole me one day 'bout a ol' Cajun near Prairieville. Dey say he's so tight, *whoo!* Dey say he squeak w'en he walk. He got a ol' store dair, too, an' you go dair an' buy ham, an' you t'ink iss fo' him, he cut it so t'in. "Well," one man say, "yeah, I bought some. You could see t'rough it."

"Well, he slices mine more t'inner den dat," say anodder Cajun.

"How you gon' slice it t'inner den dat?"

"De order he sol' me, you could only see one side."

Truck Drivers License

Well, dair was a Cajun, a truck drivin' Cajun, who haul off an' let his chauffeur license expire on him. His chauffeur license done run isse'f plum' out. He a truck-drivin' man, he can't have a ordinary drivin' license like you an' me. He got to have a chauffeur license like dat, you year?

So he walk into de place where de drivin'-license examinating man, he live dair an' he got a office dair, you know. An' he say, "Ma' frien', my chauffeur license done expire isse'f. W'at I gon' did?"

De man say, "I tole you one t'ing you ain't gon' did. Don' drove dem truck, you year?"

"Well, I unnerstood dat, but w'at I'm gon' did?"

"Like I'm tole you, don' drove dem truck an' you got to take a examinatin' an' r'at now."

"Do I got to took it r'at now? Can't I brought mase'f back tomorrow mornin' to took it?"

"Oh," de man say, "of cou'se. Hell yeah. But don' you drove dem truck."

De driver say, "I wouldn't put ma' han' on it, I tole you dat fo' sho', let alone sit down in it."

"Well, you can brought you'se'f back tomorrow mornin, dat's fine."

"You min' if I brought ma' frien' Emile wit' me, hanh?"

"Hell no, I don' mine who you brought back wit' you. You can brought you' ma-ma, you' pa-pa, you' brudder, you' sister, de whole town, but you got to took dat examinatin', yeah."

Dat truck driver say, "I'll be here wit' ma' frien' Emile."

De man say, "A'r'at."

Well, de nex' mornin' here he is, wit' his frien' Emile. He introduce Emile to dat drivin'-license examinatin' man. He say, "I wan' you to meet ma' frien' Emile."

De examinatin' man say, "I'm glad fo' you to see me."

Emile say, "I'm glad fo' you to see me, too."

Well, dey sit down in dat fron' row to take dem examinatin' an' as soon as dey sit down, *shoom,* Emile gone to sleep, an' r'at now. Dat drivin'-license man say, "W'at de matter wit' him?"

Ma' frien' say, "Not'ing, he jus' like to sleep, dass all. He sleep all de time w'en he ridin' wit' me, which is mos' o' de time. He sleep all de time. Ain't not'ing wrong wit' dat."

De man say, "No, but you got to took you' drivin'-license examinatin' an' r'at now. Firs' we got de writin' part."

Well, he took de writin' part. Den he come to de part wit' dem true an' all dem damn lie on dair, you know. He got to check dat off, which is which.

Den de examinatin' man say, "Hokay, now we got to come to de oral part."

Dat Cajun say, "W'at dat is?"

De man say, "I'm gon' ax you somet'ing an' you gon' tole me."

De Cajun say, "Hokay, go 'head an' ax me, I'm boun' to know."

Well, he ax him dis an' he tole him dis, he ax him dat an' he tole him dat. He ax him dis an' he tole him dis. He kep' ax him dat an' summore o' dis an' dat. He answer all de time an' he kep' gettin' dis an' dat all r'at, avery time.

Dat man say, "Hokay, now we come to de jus' sepose."

De Cajun say, "Jus' w'at de hell is 'jus' sepose'?"

He say, "Now you gon' lissen an' fine out 'bout dis. Shut up an' lissen."

Dat Cajun say, "Hokay."

He say, "Jus' sepose you in you' truck an' iss overload. You' truck is overload all de way, plum'. An' you brought you'se'f to one o' dem deep, deep, deep, deep hills an' you jus' can make it. You jus' barely make it to de top. You finally get to de top, an' you lavel you'se'f off an' you brought you'se'f back down. You put you' foot all de way on de acceleration, *shoom.* An' you broke de law summore. You goin' too fas'. Oh, you gettin' wit' it an' you roun' a li'l curve dair goin' down dem hill an' dair's a school bus loaded wit' chirren out in fron' wit' you. You t'row down on dem broke an' you ain't got no broke. W'at you gon' did?

He say, "I'm gon' wake Emile up."

Well, dat drivin'-license man say, "W'at in de worl' you gon' wake Emile up fo'?"

He say, "Emile ain't never seen a bad wreck in his life."

A Free Cajun Electrician

I got a frien' w'at was gon' buil' a house. An' you peoples dat are in de business, you know dat lumber is higher an' labor is even higher. An' he was talkin', "I got to buil' dis house. I got to cut avery corner w'at I can, an' I got to fine some corners to cut."

An' he was talkin' to us Cajuns an' one Cajun say, "Well, I can he'p you some."

Ma' frien' say, "W'at can you do?"

Dat Cajun say, "I'm a damn good 'lactrician."

"I didn't know dat."

"Dair's a lot you don' know 'bout me. I'll wire dat house for you."

"How much?"

"Not a damn t'ing. I'll be glad to do it."

Dat fallow say, "Hokay, dass gon' save me better den a t'ousan' dollar."

Well, dey buil' de house an' dis Cajun wire it. Dey flip on de juice an' he tell de man w'at own de house, "Go chunk dat switch an' we'll show you."

He go over dair an' *shoo, swish, shoo,* fire jus' wen' averywhere. Dey had to go chunk de main switch real quick 'cause dey 'mos' set de place on fire. He say, "I t'ought you said you knew how to wire a house. Dat you' a 'lactrician."

He say, "I am."

De fallow say, "De hell you are. Look w'at happen. 'Mos' set dis place on fire."

De Cajun say, "You chunk dat switch too damn fas'."

A Fisherman's Helper

I got a frien' w'at live down in Sout'eas' Lewisana an' he's a full-bleed Cajun. De fishin' bug came in one day an' bit him all over. An' he say, "Me, I got to go fishin'." He had never been fishin' befo'.

So he wen' an' bought a boat, a big motor fo' it, a fly rod an' a spinnin' wheel rod. It took fo' box to hol' all de equipmen' he had.

He know you ain't sepose to go fishin' by you'se'f, but he couldn't fine anybody to go wit' him excep' de town dronk. So he ax him, "You wanna go fishin' wit' me, hanh?" "Oh, hell yeah," gurgled de town dronk.

So de dronk wen' to collec' his tackle—consis' o' a bottle o' dat good ol' Cajun whiskey, Jacques Dan-yell, made in Tennessee, a bucket o' minnows, an' a fishin' pole wit' a line. Ma' frien', wit' all o' his fine gear, tried avery fishin' pole he had, an' avery kine o' bait, but he didn't get a single nibble, while de town dronk was reelin' 'em in like crazy.

Ma' frien', w'at got a big cur-ous like all us Cajun, watch de town dronk to see w'at he did. He look wit' stupefy while de dronk would pour hisse'f a big slug of Jacques Dan-yell an' empty de glass into de bait bucket. Den he poured hisse'f de nex' drink. Den he would t'row his line overboard an' *wham!* Anodder one dem big bass—mus' be five poun' easy.

"Lemme see w'at I can caught wit' you' rod," say ma' frien'. De dronk handed him de pole. He t'rew de line overboard an' *wham!* Pull in a big bass r'at now.

"An' you know w'at?" he said later. "Me, I go to took de fish off de hook, an' w'at you t'ought? Ma' dronk minnow had got him by de t'roat!"

A Solution for a Problem Drinker

I got a frien' w'at I had been hontin' wit' for many, many year an' he's f'om deep, deep, deeeep Sout' Lewisana. He's a full-bleed Cajun, not half-bleed—24 carrots, an' cabbages, too, w'atever you want to say.

An' he married a beautimous lady, a wondermous lady from up nort'—way up nort' 'roun' Shrevepo't. An' ma' frien' is a full-bleed Cajun like I'm tole you, an' he's a weekend Cat-lic. An' de wondermous lady w'at he married from way up nort' is a deep-water Baptis'. By dat I mean she don' even closet-drink, you year? An' of cou'se, dis Cajun, he like a li'l sip an' a nip avery now an' den, avery day.

She made marriage wit' him, an' he have a couple o' sips an' nips an' she say, "Don' you come in de same room wit' me, let alone get in dis bed wit' me. I can't stood de smell o' dat alcohol, anyway."

Well, he chew dem coffee beans 'cause he done had a li'l sip an' nip, an' he take so much of dat Sen-Sen he 'mos' give hisse'f sugar diabetes. He nearly wear a hole in de middle o' his tongue wit' dat essence o' peppermints.

An' las' year, we wen' dock hontin', an' like I'm tole you w'en I start off, I been hontin' wit' him for years an' years, but las' year was de firs' time we stay in de same camp wit' adjoinin' room, you know.

An' I look in de nex' room an' he in his pajamas an' I saw him pop w'at I t'ought was two capsules an' den he chew dem up. I say, "He mus' be sick an' wan' some action real fas'." Den I see him stuck somet'ing up bot' nose. An' I say, "He too sick to go in de blin'. Maybe I better go see 'bout dis."

So I walk in dair an' I say, "Ma' frien', I'm sorry you sick like hell."

"Oh," he say, "I'm not sick."

I say, "You not? You took dem medicine dair an' stuck somet'ing up you' nose."

"Oh," he say, "you know ma' ol' lady."

I say, "Oh yeah."

He say, "Dass r'at. De bes' mot'er in de worl' an' a wondermous wife. But you know how she feel 'bout ma' drinkin'."

I say, "Oh yeah."

He say, "W'at I took dair, dat was two Luden cough drops. An' w'at I stuck up bot' nose dair was Victor's salve. An' I can go in dair an' go to bed an' she can't smell not'ing but Luden cough drops an' Victor's salve."

I say, "But she ain't cheer."

He say, "I know dat. But after fifteen year, you get addicted to it, I ga-ron-tee!"

Naming the Twins

I got a young couple frien's been married 'bout five year an' dey got no chirren. An' bot sides o' de fam'ly ax, "How come you got no chirren?" 'Cause the li'l girl come f'om a fam'ly o' saventeen chirren an' the young mans come f'om a fam'ly o' a even dozen—t'irteen.

One day de girl is rush to de female women's horse-pistol in Batonh Rouge an' she had twins, a boy an' a girl—not identical, no.

All the fam'ly was dair f'om bot' sides—mus' o' been t'ree hunnert of 'em—an' each one o' dem got at leas' twenty name apiece for dem twins, an' dey raise so much hell dey got to call de state police to put 'em in de parkin' lot. An' it upset the pore li'l girl what had dem twins, an' she said, "Dair ain't but one peoples dat don' said not'ing 'bout namin' ma twins an' I'm gon' let dat peoples name dem chirren."

Her ma-ma say, "Dat's me, hanh?"

"Hell no, you had fo'ty name apiece."

"Who dat was?"

"Uncle Jean-Pierre."

"Oh, no, he don' know not'ing—he's a dropout from an idiot school. He's a plain an' simple ol' fool," dey all said. She say, "I don' care, he's gon' name my chirren."

She got anodder uncle dat's a deputy sheriff in Gonzales, twenty mile sout' o' de female women's horse-pistol, an' he's late 'cause he's been workin' on a case—Schlitz, Bobweiser, one o' dem case. He come tearin' up dat Arrow-line Highway in dat petroleum car, red light flashin', wit' de syringe on full blas'.

An' he get to dat horse-pistol an' say, "I got jus' de name for dem twins." Somebody say, "You' too late." He say, "Who name 'em? I'll put 'em in jail." Dey say, "Uncle Jean-Pierre."

"Not him, he don' know not'ing."

"We said dat."

"He's a dropout f'om an idiot school."

"We said dat."

"He's a plain an' simple ol' fool."

"We said dat."

"Well, w'at dat ol' fool name 'em?"

Somebody say, "He called de li'l girl Denise."

"I'll be damned, dat ol' fool t'ink o' a good Franch name for dat li'l girl. W'at he named de li'l boy?"

"Denephew."

The Painting Millwright

A fallow got out o' work not long ago near Bat-onh Rouge, an' he was a painter. He wanted to work, so he hired on as a millwright.

He was standin' by a ladder near a big piece of equipmen', big, big ladder. An' de supervisor walk by an' he say, "Fallow, you know how to pack a pump?"

He say, "Yeah, but not up dat ladder, I ga-ron-tee!"

I Did It

I got on de elegator. Dass dat li'l room where you stood you'se'f still an' it does all de movin' fo' you. W'en I got on dair, dair was a lady wit' a li'l boy chirren 'bout nine or eight year old. She hol' his han' real good 'cause she don' wan' to los' him, no.

An' a great big fat female woman weigh 'mos' a bale o' cotton, 510 poun', get on dem elegator an' push up ag'inst dat li'l boy chirren, an' a whole load o' conventionin' safety engineers get on dair an' overload de damn t'ing.

Well, de elegator got a automatic door on it an' it brought isse'f up to de magazine flo' an' *yooom!* De do' fly isse'f open an' dat big fat female lady woman let out a scream—*whoosh!* Tore off dat elegator, knock down twelve or 'laven o' dem safety men gettin' off so fas'!

An' averybody turn 'roun' an' look at dat li'l boy like he a sheep-killin' dog. He look 'em on de eye wit' bot' eye an' he tole 'em, "I did it, I did it, I did it. She stuck it in ma' face an' I haul off an' bit it."

Truant Officer

You know, many year ago over dair in Livingston Parish where I'm f'om, dey had a truant officer dat would get de chirren w'at play hookey. Dey had a lot o' dat back dair w'en I was comin' up. De school wasn't w'at dey are today, you know. It wasn't fun to go to school—you jus' hate it.

An' dat truant officer got to messin' 'roun' an' not tendin' wit' his business an' one day de school board call him in an' *whooo!* Boy, you talk 'bout rakin' over de coals. Dey rake him up one side an' down de same side. Dey made it sore, dey rake him so hard.

He lef' dair wit' blood in his eye 'cause he not been doin' his job good an' dey tole him, "You better do somet'ing 'bout dem chirren playin' hookey aroun' here. You de truant officer."

He walk out o' dair an' wen' to downtown in Denham Springs an' dair was a li'l boy standin' on de corner. He say, "Son, how come you ain't in school, hanh?"

De li'l boy look up an' say, "Hell, mister, I ain't but five damn year ol'."

Play Ball

Years ago in Rayne at dem bessball game, you could hear de catcher talkin' to de pitcher an' it would be real quiet until somet'ing happen. Den *kerchoom*—hell broke loose. MAN!

An' one day, Rayne was playin' Abbeville an' dey had a batter on Abbeville dat could jus' look at dat ball nearly an' los' it. An' de only t'ing he couldn't took was w'at dey used to call de outshoot, de curve.

An' I was dair one day, an' dis fallow come up to bat an' Rayne was ahead one run. Abbeville got one man on base an' dis man come up to bat—great big fallow.

De catcher say to de pitcher (you can hear him up in de stan's), he say, "Dair's dat big so-an'-so." Only he call him w'at he was. "We got to watch him, now. We don' wan' him to get on base, no.

De bes' t'ing for you to did is curve him." (Dis is in de nint' innin' an' de li'l pitcher is gettin' kine o' tired.) He say, "You year? You gonna curve him?"

Dat pitcher say, "Hell yeah, I year." Well, he rare back an' chunk dat ball an' *blam*—de hide come off it. He los' it. Dat catcher stan' up an' dat fallow is joggin' to firs' base an' he say, "Didn't you year me tole you to curve him, hanh?"

De pitcher say, "I curve him, but he wouldn't broke."

An' years ago, too, in dis same league, dair was a scout name Tony John. He's still a scout for de Dodgers. An' he an' anodder scout had a boy in min' who was in high school playin' semi-pro ball, tryin' to get into de Evangeline League.

An' dey wen' to a game dat was hotly contes', you know, big rivalry between towns 'bout sixteen mile 'part. An' dey wen' dair to scout dis boy. Dey had been talkin' to de manager 'bout him an' de manager was proud o' him. He was his son—hell, he boun' to be proud o' him. An' dey snuck in. Dey didn't want de boy to know dat dey was dair.

Tony John an' dis odder scout get dair an' dey lean up ag'inst de gran'stan', an' dis boy is at bat. De manager is over on t'ird base an' he see dese scouts come over dair an' he lef' t'ird base an' walk over dair an' squat down to talk wit' dem. An' de empire, who live in de odder town, holler, "You' out." An' de boy hadn't even struck at de ball yet.

Dat manager jomp up an' say, "W'at you said?"

He say, "De batter's out, I ga-ron-tee."

"W'at de hell you mean he's out? He ain't got a strike or a ball too on him either!"

"Jus' like I tole you, de batter is out."

"How come he's out?"

"You talkin' to de scout, dat's how come he's out."

"Where do you get dat?"

"From de rule book."

De manager say, "Get dat rule book. I want to see dat rule book you talkin' 'bout."

Dat li'l empire beat hisse'f on de ches' an' say, "You lookin' at de rule book."

Topics of Conversation

I fly out of New Or-lee-anhs several time a week an' I been doin' it a good many years, an' I go t'rough de marvelous li'l city of Laplace. Dey got a wondermous res'rant dair call de Airline Motors Res'rant—real fine food, an' I been stoppin' dair for years 'cause dey got dat food, an' you can look at me an' tole I eat mos' o' it.

An' I got to know mos' averybody in Laplace. One day I wen' t'rough dair an' I saw a frien' wit' me. He say, "Hey, Juice-tanh, where de hell you been?"

"I been t'rough here four time a week. Where de hell you been you'se'f?" I say.

"Oh," he say, "dass r'at. Well, I'm workin' on one dem dredger boat. We got to keep de cha-nel open fo' de traffic." He say, "We go out dair early Monday mornin', an' we don' got back 'til late Friday. Juice-tanh, you know w'at dem Cajuns talk 'bout all week long in dat dredger boat, hanh?"

I say, "I got a good idea."

"Dass r'at. *Women, women, women, women.* But w'en we got sho' Friday, dey rush to de neares' barroom saloon an' all dey talk 'bout is dredger boat, dredger boat, dredger boat!"

The Hunting Expedition

Not long ago, I got a frien' name Wayne Picou who lives down sout' o' me 'bout eighteen or saventeen mile in a area w'at we call Bear Islan' section o' Maurepas, swamp town. An' he got a grocery store an' he work hard, but he love to hont, too.

An' one day, one o' dem city-slickin' Cajun from aroun' Bat-onh Rouge or someplace like dat say, "Wayne, you know you ain't never ax me to go squirrel hontin' wit' you." (Now, dis was las' September.)

Wayne say, "I ain't never ax you to go squirrel hontin' wit' me?"

He say, "Dat's r'at."

Wayne say, "Well, how come you don' go squirrel hontin' wit' me?"

He say, "Well, I'm glad you ax me. I'll be glad to did dat."

Wayne say, "We can't go now. De season close." He didn't tole him he been goin' by hisse'f. He say, "De season open two Sattiday from now. You met me at ma' house befo' daylight an' we'll go hont dem squirrel."

He say, "Hokay, I'll be dair."

Two Sattidays from den at 2 a.m. o'clock in de mornin', *beep, beep, beeeep.* Wayne go out dair an' say, "Who de hell dat is dis time o' night, hanh? Who blowin' de horn like dat?"

De city slicker say, "Well, you tole me to get cheer befo' daylight."

Wayne say, "But, hell, I didn't mean fo' you to come yestiddy." He say, "You year. Come on, brought you'se'f in an' we'll make some breakfas' an' some coffee an' den we'll go get dem squirrel."

So he brought hisse'f in an' dey made some coffee an' dey made some breakfas' an' dey wait a li'l while. Dèn dey get in Wayne Picou's jeep 'cause de road ain't some good in dat swamp. An' dem frogs is *kerump, kerump, kerump,* jus' givin' it a good goin' over, you know.

An' dey in dat jeep an' dey go to de en' o' de road by de Black Lake Club. W'en I'm talk 'bout de en' o' de road, all you can hear an' you can't see is *kerump, kerump, kerump, kerump,* dem frogs jus' raisin' hell.

An' dey wait 'til daylight. An' it been dry but not too dry. W'en it got daylight, dis city-slickin' Cajun from Bat-onh Rouge say, "I ain't goin' in dat swamp an' hont no squirrels, no."

Wayne say, "Well, you got to. You can't got dem on de highway an' on de road."

He say, "I ain't goin' in dair."

Wayne say, "How come you ain't goin' in dair?"

He say, "Mus' be ten million—at leas' ten million—snake in dair. I ain't goin' in dair." An' it was hot weat'er an' he was tellin' jus' 'bout de trut', maybe missin' one or two snake.

Wayne say, "Look, dair ain't snake number one in dair."
He say, "You' crazy."
Wayne say, "No, I ain't. I'll ga-ron-tee dat dair ain't snake number one in dair."
Dat Cajun say, "How can you ga-ron-tee dat?"
Wayne say, " 'Cause de alley-gators done et 'em all up."

Out of Gas

Down in Sout' Lewisana dair is a small horse-pistol dat is run by a group o' nuns. Bleeve me w'en I tell you dat dey run a jam-up horse-pistol, 'cause I spen' twenty-one mont' in one an' dey were great. Dey save ma' life, I ga-ron-tee.

An' las' year, dey had one rough time. Dey had de Asian flu, dey had de Cajun flu, all kine o' flu. Dey work all day, 24 hour a day. Finally, spring brought isse'f an' dey begin to slack off a li'l bit.

An' one day, de Mot'er Superior called dem in an' she say, "Sisters, I know you been havin' a bad time. So I'm tole you w'at I want you to did. I want you to go on a picnic—not on de groun's. Go to a li'l bayou or creek. Get away from here an' have you'se'ves a good time."

Dey all say, "T'ank you, Mot'er."

So dey fry schicken, make potato salad, boil aggs, an' get ready fo' dat picnic.

Dey get out on de interstate an' dey done scheck averyt'ing but the gas register of dat ol' stationary wagon dat dey got. An' it not long befo' dey hear putt-putt-putt-putt, an' dat ol' stationary wagon come to a dead still.

One o' dem nuns say, "Well, accordin' to de gas register, we is out o' gas."

Anodder say, "I'm a pretty good mechanic, an' I can tole by de way it soun'—we is out o' gas."

But dey could see one o' dem tall, tall sign fo' a fullin' station on up ahead not too far. So one o' dem say, "I'll go up dair an' get jus' enuf fo' us to get dair an' full up. Fine me somet'ing to put some gas in."

So dey rummage t'rough dat stationary wagon an' all dey could fine was a bedpan. Well, de sister took dat an' go to de fullin' station. An' in jus' a li'l while, she come back, real careful not to spill any of dat gas.

Dey was standin' dair puttin' it in when one o' dese tandem trailin' trucks come by. De driver see w'at goin' on an' he put on dat air-broke, *shoooo,* an' he brought dat truck to a stop an' r'at now. He back up to dem an' he say, "Sister, I'm sorry, but I jus' don' bleeve dat gon' work. But I got to tell you dis, Sister, I sho' do admire you' faith."

The Winless Candidate

Dair is an ol' fallow down in Ascension Parish dat fo' de las' six time has run for de justice o' de peace. An' he ain't never won anyt'ing in his life. Dis is de six time he was runnin' for justice o' de peace summore. Iss not a vary big office, but iss certain duties we mus' have unner de Lewisana law.

A frien' o' mine name Mac DeArmond one day say, "Hello, ma' frien'," an' de ol' man say, "Hello, Mac, you gon' vote for me dis time?"

An' Mac say, "W'at you runnin' fo'?"

He say, "Ma' same ol' job."

The Reluctant Student

Year befo' las' dair was a young couple down in de li'l town where I live dat had a li'l boy chirren dat wen' to school fo' de firs' time an' dey tole me 'bout him.

He wen' to school dat firs' day an' he did not wan' to go. All dis new eddication did not appeal to him none a-tall any. Man, his ma-ma had to whip him to make him go to school. An' he finally wen'.

An' he come home from school dat day an' he play til he jus' wore plum' out. De nex' mornin' his ma-ma woke him up an' he say, "W'at you woke me up fo', Ma-ma? I'm tired. I jus' play so hard yestiddy evenin'."

She say, "You got to go to school."

He say, "I done been."

The Lost Wallet

I got a frien' w'at was sheriff over in dat wonderful parish of St. Landry. Iss a free state, I ga-ron-tee. He say, "One day I got a call w'en I was at de office dair f'om a li'l fallow an' he say, 'Look, will you min' sen' somebody over year? Somebody done stole ma' wal-let, ma' pock-ett book.'

"So I sen' de deputy an' we go over dair an' wen' in dair an' dis young fallow was dair in dis roadhouse.

"An' I say, 'Son, are you sho' dat you didn't come out o' dis place some a-tall none any?' He say, 'I didn't lef' de place. I was over dair in one o' dem boot', sittin' at dem table, tendin' wit' ma' own business, an' ma' wal-let gone, ma' pock-ett book gone.'

"You know, we turn dem place upside down, turn dem boot' up, wen' behin' de bar, took de rug up f'om de flo' an' look beneat' dat, an' we didn't fine no wal-let.

"An' I say, 'Son, I wan' to ax you somet'ing. Have you look in all you' pock-etts?'

"An' he say, 'All but one.'

"I say, 'How come you ain't look dair?'

"He say, 'It may not be dair.' "

A New Kind of Plow Horse

Dair's a ol' couple live near Gonzales—dass de gumbo capital o' de worl', I wan' you to know—an' de only pension w'at dey got is social security. An' dey get by real good on dat, 'cause dey always have a fine garden dat dey plant. An' dey plow dat garden wit' a mule dat dey got an' had a long time. Dey can a lot o' stuff an' dey freeze a lot o' stuff an' man, dey got all dey want to eat an' dey raise a couple o' calf avery year an' dey butcher dat an' dey freeze dat, too.

An' las' spring, de ol' lady tole de ol' man, "Look, we got to get de garden plow up." He say, "Don' worry 'bout dat. I'll plow de damn garden w'en iss time to did dat."

Well, avery day she say, "W'en you gon' plow dem garden?" He say, "I'll get aroun' to it. Don' worry some any a-tall none."

Well, one day he say, "I'm gon' go plow dem garden," an' he wen' outside to go hitch up dem mule an' he come back in de house an' she say, "I t'ought you was gon' go plow dem garden."

He say, "Well, I can't did dat. Dat damn ol' mule done haul off an' drop dead."

She say, "You see dair? I tole you to plow dem garden an' you ain't did dat. How we gon' plow de garden? We ain't gon' have no garden. You did not plow de garden."

She didn't tole him dat once a day, no. Not one hunnert, too. Ten t'ousan' time in t'ree days. Oh, she rake him up one side an' down de odder, made it raw. Oh, she give him a goin' over. "You see dair, you didn't plow de garden. Now we ain't gon' have no garden. You didn't plow de garden."

He say, "Hitch me up. I'll plow dat damn garden."

She say, "A'r'at, less go."

Dey got out dair an' she hitch him up. She got dat singletree, got dem trace chains, an' she rig him up good. She put dat bridle on dair an' put dem line aroun' her shoulder an' grab dem plow handle dair an' crack dat whip an' "Ye-hah! Git up dair."

Well, man, he pull an' he strain an' he pull an' she tryin' to push him, too, to he'p him 'long. An' he get to de headlan' an' he run into de briars, run into a barb-wire fence an' thresh 'roun' an' stomble all over.

She say, "W'at in de worl' de matter wit' you?"

He say, "Don' you know how to holler *'Whoa'*?"

Mail Call

I got to tole you a true story 'bout somet'ing dat happen near where I live. A few fire distric's were established down dair, an' dey got a call one day dat dair was a fire down de new blacktop road dey got dair.

De shiny new fire truck wen' roarin' down de road. Red lights an' blue lights goin' blinkety, blinkety, blink. De sheriff's car was r'at behin'. But dey didn't saw no smoke. An' de driver slow down an' yell to de chief, "I didn't saw no smoke." But de chief yell, "Keep goin'. Sounds good!"

A few minnits later de road began to play out. At de same time, dey spy a man by de side o' de road wavin' like crazy.

"Where's de fire?" yell de chief.

De excited man stoodin' by de road dair yell back, "I don' know, but would you mail dese two letters for me w'en you got back to town?"

Determined Deer Hunter

I live in Livingston Parish, an' a Livingston Parish deer honter is different from all de odder deer honter in de worl'. He work construction so he can take all deer season off. He loves to hont dem deers.

I got a frien' w'at is a real, for true, hones' Livingston Parish deer honter. An' he met a good-lookin' female girl lady woman live way up nort', 'roun' Shrevepo't. An' he courted her real good all spring an' in June dey made marriage.

She didn't know not'ing 'bout dem Livingston Parish deer honter. Come November he say, "I'm goin' to hont dem deers."

She say, "W'at you said?"

He say, "I'm goin' to hont dem deers."

"Don' you ree-lize you a marriage man?"

"Not dem kinda deers, dese de kine wit' antling."

She say, "I'm goin' witcha."

He say, "I'll be damned, iss not'ing but a dirty ol' men's camp an' you can't go."

Well, she bawled an' squalled and raise some sand, but he went to hont dem deers. Six week later he come back and she so glad to see him she don' run him off. One day she say, "I'm gon' have a bêbe."

"I'll make a deer honter out o' him."

"It might be a girl."

"Oh, no, iss gon' be a boy."

She had de bêbe, a fine, healt'y boy. An' she fo'got all 'bout dem deers. But come November he say, "I'm goin' to hont dem deers."

"W'at 'bout de bêbe?"

"He's too young to go."

She bawled and squalled and raise some sand, but he went to hont dem deers.

The nex' year she got her ma-ma from up nort' come stay wit' her an' in November he say, "I'm goin' to hont dem deers." She say, "I'm goin' witcha." He say, "I'll be damned, iss a dirty ol' men's camp wit' no sanitary faculties. You can't go." She say, "Look, if I don' go witcha to hont dem deers, when you get back we be gone, me, Ma-ma, an' de bêbe, an' you ain't never gon' see us again." He say, "O.K., but we got to get you a shootgun." She say, "I got one a'ready an' I been practicin' to shot dat t'ing."

Dey go to de camp an' de nex' mornin' he say, "I axed de game warden an' he say dat I can took de plug out you gun an' you can shot any kine o' deers, a female doe deer or a male buck deer, it don' make some diff'rence. You got five buck-shoot shells an' I'm gon' be on a stan' 'bout 100 yard away so you don' got to worry about a t'ing." She say, "Don' worry you'se'f, I'll be r'at cheer."

He didn't got fifty yard when he hear *bloom, bloom, bloom, bloom, bloom.* "Great balls o' fire, she done kill a deer an' I don' even got to ma stan'. Dey gon' cut my shirttail off fo' sho'."

He start runnin' back an' de more closer he got, he hear a big argue. "Don' you put you' han' on ma deer or I'll blow a hole in you dat I can walk t'rough. Don' you lay a finger on ma deer." She is reloadin' dat gun.

He part de weeds an' she had dat gun pointed on a man. "Don' you touch ma deer," she say.

"Lady," de man say, "I'm not gon' touch you deer, but you min' if I get ma saddle off him, hanh?"

Wrong Way to Illustrate

Savarel year ago, I was doin' a lot of safety work for machine shops all over de country, an' dair was a Cajun work in one o' dem name Andre. Funny? *Whoo!* He was funny, yeah. Do anyt'ing fo' a laugh or a surprise. He work on a lathe, a metal lathe, an' one day I wen' dair to see if Andre had any new stories.

He wasn't dair, an' I ax some people dair, I say, "Where is Andre?" Dey say, "He home. He had a axident, him. He cut his finger off on a lathe. He won't be back for six week, plum'."

"How de hell did he did dat, hanh?"

"We don' know."

I was back to see Andre six week later. I wanted to fine out how de hell he cut his finger off on a metal lathe.

I walk up to Andre an' say, "Andre, how you are?" He turn hisse'f 'roun' an' say, "Hello, Juice-tanh, I'm fine, an' how are you?"

"I unnerstood you cut you' finger off."

"Dass r'at," he say. "Look." An' he show me de nub where de finger had been.

"How de hell did you did dat?" I ax him.

He say, "Jus' like dis, Juice-tanh," an' he stuck anodder finger unner de metal lathe jus' to show me how it was did.

Surprises by the Numbers

You know, I got t'ree frien's w'at was in de female womens horse-pistol in Bat-onh Rouge in de waitin' room waitin' fo' dey wives. An' I don' mean groceries, no. De nurse came out an' said, "Mr. Boudreaux, you got twins, a girl an' a boy. Fine, healt'y chirren."

After he gulp once or twice an' caught his breathe, he say, "Well, iss only fit an' proper dat I should have twins. I'm chief scout fo' de Minnesota Twins bessball team in Sout'wes' Lewisana." He turn aroun' an' han' two seegars to each o' de two expactant fat'ers stoodin' dair.

Pretty soon de same nurse was brought herse'f out dair. She say, "Mr. Bourgeois?" One o' dem mans pass a big grin on his look an' he say, "Hey, bêbe. Here I am, me, r'at cheer. W'at I got?"

"You got more den two," she say.

"W'at you said?"

"Oh yeah," she say, "you got t'ree wonderful bêbes. Iss two fine, healt'y girls an' a boy."

"You don' mean to tole me. Dass marvelous. Well, iss only fit dat I should have triplets. I represent de 3-M Company in Lewisana. Iss fit an' proper dat I should have triplets."

De las' man say, "Lemme got outta here. I work fo' de 7-Up Company."

D.W.E.G.

Peoples always ax me, "Where do you got your stories?" An' I tole dem, "It's de Cajuns." Week befo' las' ma' good frien' Walter Guithreaux, live down on de bayou, telephone me at 5:30 a.m. in de mornin' an' he say, "Juice-tanh?" I say, "W'at de trouble?"

He say, "Man, one o' our good frien's jus' got pick up."

I say, "Who?"

He say, "Charlie Cahn got pick up."

I say, "Oh, w'at for?"

He say, "For D.W.E.G."

I say, "W'at de hell is D.W.E.G.?"

He say, "Drivin' while eatin' gumbo."

A Retriever Named Phideaux

I got a frien' w'at live down in Crowley, Lewisana, an' he had made his crop loan an' averyt'ing, an' he had mortgaged averyt'ing he owned excep' a retrievin' dog named Phideaux. An' he t'ought of a bankin' peoples in Stuttgart, Arkansas, who might len' him $2500 on Phideaux, de vary bes' huntin' dog in de worl' an de U., S., an' A., too.

So he wen' up to see dem bankin' peoples, an' he tol' him, "Me, I need $2500 bad, an' I brought ma' collaterals wit' me."

De bankin' peoples say, "W'at kine o' collaterals you got dair, hanh?"

He say, "Ma' retrievin' dog name Phideaux, de vary bes'."

De bankin' peoples say, "Lemme see Phideaux perform." So dey wen' out to a pon' an' sen' Phideaux ahead. He come back an' bark six time. Ma' frien' say, "Dair's six duck on dat pon' up dair."

Dis bankin' peoples f'om Stuttgart, one o' dem disbleevers, say, "Me, I don' bleeve it, no." He say, "Less go see." So dey crawl on dey belly like a alley-gator, an' w'en dey got dair, dey look, an' dair's six dock.

Dis bankin' peoples say, "Axident. Less try anodder pon'." Dey fin' anodder pon', sen' ol' Phideaux ahead, an' he come back an' bark 'laven time, an' sho' enuf, dair is 'laven dock dair.

Dis bankin' peoples say, "Me, I'm a bleever. I'll loan you de money. I got a big shoot f'om way up nort'—Memphis—gon' brought hisse'f here nex' week. I'm gon' put de bee on him good, 'cause I need a lot o' money an' he love dem dock."

Ma' frien' say, "Hokay, here is Phideaux, an' took good care of him."

He didn't hear not'ing f'om de bankin' peoples fo' t'ree mont', an' one day he ran into him an' ax him how Phideaux was doin'. "Oh," he say, "I had to kill dat dog."

"W'at you said?"

"I had to kill dat dog. I shot his head off."

"W'at happen?"

"Well, like I'm tole you, I got dat big shoot down dair, an' we took Phideaux hontin' wit' us. We sen' him on ahead. He ran back, pick up a stick an' beat it in ma' leg. Den he run at dem big shoot an' beat *him* on de leg wit' de stick. It scared hell out o' dat big Memphis shoot an' he holler, 'Dat dog has gone plum' mad. Kill dat damn dog.'

"*Bloom.* I shot his head off."

"Oh," ma' frien' say, "you made a terrible mistook. Dat dog was jus' tryin' to tole you dair were more dock up ahead den you could shook a stick at."

The Sick Cajun

I never will fo'got savarel year ago, 'bout t'ree or two o'clock in de mornin', I got a ol' frien' who woke up an' he had some real bad ches' pains. In fac', he was havin' a heart attack, dat's w'at was happenin' wit' him. His wife heard him moanin' an' groanin' an' she wake up, too. An' he was up dair, 'bout 83 or 82 year ol'. She say, "W'at de matter, Pa-pa?"

He say, "I feel bad."

She say, "I'll call de doc-taire."

He say, "No, don' call de doc-taire. We ain't got none o' de ol' doc-taire lef'. Dey done all retire or pass away an' dem young doc-taire don' know not'ing."

"Oh," she say, "I got to call."

He say, "No, ooh wheeeee." An' he feel real bad.

She say, "I'm gon' call one." So she pick up de foam an' call. She say, "Dr. Boudreaux, dis is Mrs. Broussard. Will you please come quick? Pa-pa is sick, sick, sick."

Well, young Dr. Boudreaux come over an' r'at now. He didn't live far an' he jus' chunk on a pair of pants wit' his pajamas an' he had his black bag. He walk over to de bed an' say, "Mr. Broussard, tell me where you hurt, hanh?"

Broussard look up at him an' say, "You de doc-taire. You tole me where I hurt."

"Oh," he say, "come on, Mr. Broussard, tell me where you

hurt. I may be able to he'p you dair."

He say, "No, jus' like I tole Ma-ma, you young doc-taire don' know not'ing. *You* tole *me* where I hurt."

Dr. Boudreaux say, "Mrs. Broussard, will you call Dr. Melancon an' tole him to come over here an' consult wit' me on dis case?"

She say, "Dr. Melancon?"

He say, "Dat's r'at."

Broussard say, "Wait jus' a minnit, Doc. Dr. Melancon—ain't dat de veternarian, hanh?"

De doc say, "Dat's r'at. Dat's de vet a'r'at. An' dass de only doc-taire in town dat I know of dat can look a jackass in de face an' tell where he hurt."

Savoir-Faire

You know, avery once in a while you hear somet'ing dat will remin' you of a story you tole many year ago, an' I tole dis story I ain't gon' tole you how many year ago. It been a long, long time, I ga-ron-tee.

You know, w'en all de boys start to brought deyse'fs home f'om all de countries f'om all over de worl' dat dey had been sent to an' lef', dey pick up all kine o' phrases an' words from dese varied lands an' countries. An' dey brought 'em back home wit' dem. An' w'en dey got back home, dey would use dem words an' phrases an' dere wifes couldn't unnerstood w'at dey was talkin' 'bout. Dey t'ought dey was tryin' to get away wit' somet'ing an' dey wasn't doin' dat.

So 'bout fo' or t'ree agghaid up nort'—someplace in Massachusetts where dey got dem junior colleges, you know—decide dat w'at dey should do is make a bran' new dictionair an' get all dese words an' phrases dat dey bring back and give a short simple define so de peoples would know w'at in de worl' dey were talkin' 'bout.

So dey haul off an' did dat. Dey start makin' dat dictionair dair, an' dey didn't have no trouble wit' Chinese, Sanscrip, Arabic,

German, Swedish, Russian, or Hungarian, an' dey didn't have much trouble wit' Anglish. An' dey did jus' fine wit' Franch until dey come to one phrase an' dey could not, all fo' of 'em, agree on a short define, even wit' fo' or t'ree pages like dey got in dis new American Heritage Dictionair. After dey wrote fo' or t'ree pages, dey still did not have no real good simple define or axample of w'at in de worl' dis Franch phrase mean.

An de phrase was vary simple: "savoir faire." De Franch phrase "savoir faire." Well, one o' dem had not been ruin' completely, he still had a li'l common sense lef'. He say, "How come we don' talk to a Franchman dair in America who is a American Franchman?"

One o' dem odder ones say, "Where you gon' fine dat?" *Whoo!* He a edicatted fool! Dat firs' one say, "We can fine dat in Louisiana. Dey got a lot o' American Franchmen down dair. Less call 'em an' go down dair an' see 'em."

De odders say, "Hokay."

So dey call de superintendent of schools down in Lewisana, an' he say, "Well, I'll be glad to talk wit' you-all, Professor, and I'll get de supervisor an' de principal o' de school so we can come up wit' anyt'ing you would like." Dis was in Livingston Parish.

So dey all get toget'er an' de professor say, "Look, we got to have a short, simple define an' a axample of de phrase 'savoir faire.' Can you do dat?"

De superintendent of de schools say, "Why, sho', I can do dat. Now you take me. I work pretty hard, but I leave about fo'-t'irty in de evenin' an' go to my home an' I walk in dair one evenin'. An' I walk in my livin' room, my parlor, an' dair is my wife sittin' on de couch wit' anodder man, kissin' him—kissin' dat odder man. An' I tip my hat an' say, ' 'Scuse me, please.' Dat's savoir faire."

De supervisor o' de schools say, "It broke ma' heart to dispute de word of ma' 'mediate superior, but dass not quite r'at, no. I work a li'l bit longer an' I don' get in 'til 'bout five-t'irty in de evenin'. An' I go home an' walk in ma' livin' room, in ma' parlor, an' I see ma' wife sittin' on de couch wit' anodder man, kissin' dat odder man. An' I tip ma' hat an' say, ' 'Scuse me, please. Continue you'se'f.' Dat's savoir faire."

Well, de principal o' de school say, "I mos' probably gon' los' ma' job, but I got to dispute de word o' ma' 'mediate superior an' ma' mediate superior 'mediate superior, an' it broke ma' heart to did dat. But take me, now. I don' get home 'til 'bout saven-t'irty in de evenin', 'cause I got to help de coach wit' de football team. An' w'en I get home, I walk in ma' livin' room, an' dair's ma' wife sittin' on de couch, kissin' anodder man. An' I walk in an' I tip ma' hat, an' I say, ' 'Scuse me, please. Continue you'se'f.' An' if he can continue hisse'f, *he* got savoir faire."

The Biographer

Savarel year ago, dair was a lady female women schoolteacher teachin' Anglish. You can tell how long ago dat was—today dey call it language. An' she had a li'l boy in her classroom name Tijon, an' he had a terrible aggravatin' habit of not bein' able to say somet'ing in a few words. She ax him a question an' he had to answer a full page. She tole him to write a t'eme or t'esis—how-you-call a hessay—an' it look like *Gone Wit' the Win'.* Look a foot t'ick. Took her fo' day to read de damn t'ing an' he could wrote it overnight.

She say, "I got to broke him o' dis kine o' stuff. He got to be able to tole somebody somet'ing in a few words. He got to be able to wrote a sho't paragraph. He'll never be able to go to work for de AP or de UPI."

So one day she say, "Now, Tijon, don' you said not'ing. You jus' nod you' head if you unnerstood w'at I'm talk 'bout. I want you to bring in a sho't, sho't biography of Benjamin Franklin. You unnerstood dat?" He nod his head.

"An' I want to tole you r'at now, it got to be sho't, sho't or you done waste a whole year in dis Anglish class. You unnerstood dat, hanh?" He nod his head.

De nex' day, he brought hisse'f in an' she say, "Tijon, did you wrote a sho't, sho't biography of Benjamin Franklin?"

He say, "No, I wrote a sho't, sho't, sho't, sho't, sho't . . ."

She say, "Never min'. Stan' up an' read de damn t'ing."

So he stan' hisse'f up, hol' up his paper, an' he read, "Benjamin Franklin born in Boston, move to Philadelphia. Dair he met a female girl lady womans. She laff at him. Later on he marry dis female girl lady womans an' discover 'lactricity."